PSYCHOLOGY OF JUVENILE CRIME

PSYCHOLOGY OF JUVENILE CRIME

Amy Lamson, Ph.D.

Private Practice,
Psychiatry and Law Center
San Diego, California

HUMAN SCIENCES PRESS, INC.
72 Fifth Avenue
NEW YORK, NY 10011

Printed in the United States of America
23456789 987654321

Library of Congress Cataloging in Publication Data

Lamson, Amy.

    Psychology of juvenile crime.

    Bibliography: p.
    Includes index.
    1. Juvenile delinquents--Psychology. 2. Juvenile
delinquency. I. Title. [DNLM: 1. Juvenile delinquency--
Psychology. WS 462 L241p]
HV9069.L25   364.3'6'019   82-3017
ISBN 0-89885-060-6   AACR2

CONTENTS

INTRODUCTION

In my work as a clinical psychologist consultant to a juvenile probation department I am requested to evaluate juvenile offenders and make recommendations as to their suitable treatment and placement. I approach each case much like a detective. But instead of trying to figure out who did the crime, I try to figure out why it was done. What were the factors in this person's background that enabled him or her to commit the crime? What were the immediate precipitants of the crime? Then, before making a recommendation regarding disposition, I also consider the seriousness of the crime, the history, if any, of prior offenses and how they were handled, the strengths and weaknesses of the offender, the ability of the family to make changes needed to prevent future acting-out behavior, and finally, the rehabilitation and treatment resources available in the community.

At first each case was a unique puzzle to me, but after a while certain patterns began to emerge. Some cases seemed to be primarily a subcultural expression. Others seemed to reflect deep psychological problems. Still others seemed related to genetic, neurological, or psychological developmental insufficiencies. As the patterns became clearer and clearer, I developed the idea of presenting them in a book to help others identify and appropriately deal with psychological problems leading to criminal behavior in the young.

In the case of parents, teachers, counselors, and therapists, it is hoped that increased awareness of these problems will help ward off criminal behavior in potential offenders. In the case of probation officers, lawyers, and judges, it is hoped that this material will be useful in arriving at suitable dispositions for offenders whose criminal behavior is due primarily to psychological problems or developmental inadequacies, in contrast to offenders whose criminal behavior is primarily related to a delinquent subculture.

Since all the material in this book is based on clinical observations, insights, and judgments, no statistical data are presented. However, this categorization of juvenile offenders may raise questions that statistically minded researchers might want to investigate.

Chapter 2 is a survey of research on juvenile delinquency. Chapter 3 discusses the significance of school adjustment in juvenile delinquency. Chapter 4 discusses the rationale and effectiveness of various rehabilitation efforts. Chapters 5 through 14 deal with particular psychological patterns underlying criminal behavior. These chapters are arranged in approximate order of increasing psychological impairment. While each juvenile offender usually exhibits some combination of these patterns, it is possible to categorize offenders by their major characteristics and thereby determine the general level of psychological functioning. Finally, Chapter 15 deals with patterns of behavior in parents of juvenile offenders.

Chapter 1

RESEARCH ON CAUSES
OF JUVENILE DELINQUENCY

Historical Overview

Historically, sociologists have been more involved than psychologists in the study of juvenile delinquency. As a result, public discussions have focused on the social conditions in urban, industrialized societies that are most strongly associated with juvenile crime, including low income, substandard schooling, deteriorating neighborhoods, lack of recreational facilities, and exposure to criminal activities. Although criminologic research demonstrates that these conditions are linked to a higher rate of delinquency than exists in materially more advantaged environments, it has also become obvious that these social conditions are neither sufficient nor necessary explanations of juvenile delinquency. Many youngsters growing up in materially disadvantaged environments manage to avoid delinquent involvement while many youngsters growing up in materially advantaged environments seek out delinquent companions and activities.

These observations have caused sociologists to shift their attention to more specific environmental factors precipitating juvenile crime, in particular, homes broken by parental death, desertion, or divorce. But here again it has become obvious that while there is much evidence that these situations are related to a higher incidence of delinquency, they are neither sufficient nor necessary explanations. Many delinquents come from intact families and many youngsters from nonintact families grow up perfectly law abiding. Besides, the relationship between broken homes and delinquency is not entirely clear. Andrew (1978) reported: "Some authorities have found the intact family may, under some circumstances, produce more violence than the broken family." Andrews examined family variables for 214 delinquents and discovered: "The most violent delinquents were males from large intact homes." She concluded: "The pathogenicity of the large intact family for males may be difficult to recognize because of cultural bias." Eagly and Anderson (1974) suggested that the large intact families may evoke stereotyped sex roles, including violence in males. Robins, West, and Herjanic (1975) suggested that having a pathological father may be more damaging than having no father at all.

Evidently, it is necessary to go beyond the bare statistics, beyond the formal structure of families, to study the quality of parenting and the interactional patterns in these families, including supervision, discipline, and emotional warmth. But even that is not enough. The fact that very often children in the same family exhibit widely differing behavior points to the necessity of also studying the inner workings of juvenile offenders to understand specific personality factors entering into their delinquent behavior.

These realizations have prompted psychologists to join sociologists in the investigation of juvenile delinquency. The word "join" is very apt even though sociologists and psychologists approach the phenomenon from opposite ends of the spectrum—the former focusing on societal factors, the latter focusing on individual factors—with the family as the midpoint and common meeting ground between the two. It is obvious that neither field has all the answers; both have valid contributions to make. Moreover, a full understanding of the phenomenon depends upon the integration of insights from both, in much the same way that individual functioning cannot be explained by a summation of separate variables, but instead requires a holistic understanding of mind-body, self-other interactions.

The following review of the literature on juvenile delinquency is intended to highlight major research approaches and findings.

Defining Juvenile Delinquency

The most basic research on this subject is defining the phenomenon. In their 1961 book, *Measuring Delinquency*, Eaton and Polk indicated that the average delinquent is not dangerous. "Slightly less than ⅓ conformed to the 'criminal model.' Slightly more than ⅓ involved unacceptable impulse expression and about another ⅓ involved minor violations." Moreover, "the formal charge against a youngster has little diagnostic utility in determining why the youngster is in trouble or what should be done to rehabilitate him. It is more descriptive of the community context in which it occurred." Lewis (1976) concurred that "the severity of the offense is not necessarily a reliable measure of severe psychopathy."

In line with Eaton and Polk's observation that less than one-third of juvenile offenders are true criminals, many researchers, e.g. Friday and Halsey (1977), reported that the majority of juvenile delinquents grow up to be law-abiding adults.

In their 1940 book, *Juvenile Delinquents Grown Up*, Glueck and Glueck compared reformed and nonreformed delinquents on numerous background variables. They concluded:

> Those who abandoned their criminalistic behavior were more favorably endowed and raised in better circumstances than those who continued. . . . Earlier reformation of some offenders may be accounted for by their better innate equipment, early environment, more intelligent discipline by parents and the apparently helpful effect of earlier arrest and contact with the juvenile court [relative to the onset of delinquent behavior]. In other words, there is a better chance of stopping delinquency if it is "nipped in the bud."

Lewis (1976) pointed out: "The younger the age of the child at the first offense, the greater the likelihood of larger numbers of subsequent offense, the greater the likelihood of larger numbers of subsequent offenses and the greater the likelihood that psychiatric treatment would be required in adulthood."

In a study of the relative effectiveness of probation vs. detention for different types of delinquents, Saunders and Davies (1976) found: "Most of the scales [on the Jesness inventory] that predicted failure in the sample of probationers also predicted failure with the detention centre boys. This suggests that the same type of offender is succeeding both on probation and at the detention centre." The neurotic juvenile offenders are most likely to stop their delinquent behavior. The unsocialized, aggressive, antiauthority, unempathic boys are most likely to continue in their delinquencies.

According to the Gluecks, maturation is the chief explanation of the improvements shown, but this normal process is retarded by poorer resources. Offenders whose criminality is due primarily to adverse influences rather than any deepseated personal weakness eventually outgrow their delinquencies. In contrast, those with innate and early conditioned deficiencies continue to be criminal until later years when they "burn out" due to a loss of energy and aggressiveness. However, as already indicated, there is mounting evidence that this population is likely to have serious psychiatric problems in later life (Lewis, 1976).

Crimogenic Factors

The next most basic research involves searching for causal factors. Dudycha, in the chapter on juvenile delinquency in his 1955 book, *Psychology for Law Enforcement Officers*, pointed out the necessity of looking for a pattern of factors in delinquency, rather than a single cause. Accordingly, he grouped numerous factors under the following subheadings: social, physical, psychological, and conflict within the home. His social factors include culture conflict between generations, as well as the usual sociological findings related to poverty. The physical factors listed were glandular conditions, physical defects, diseases, and brain injuries. His psychological factors dealt with faulty learning patterns and conflicts between drives and society. Under conflict within the home he cited stability of the home, the parent-child relationship, and excessive parental permissiveness or domination. One of Dudycha's most interesting observations was that delinquent activities "indicate a desire to escape from restraint, experience adventure, or find oblivion in the group.... [in situations where]...homelife is dull, emotionally cold, or full of conflict."

General Psychological Findings Related to Criminal Causation

Shore's 1971 article, "Psychological Theories of the Causes of Antisocial Behavior," is the most comprehensive and intensive study of criminal causation in the literature to date. The main points will be summarized here, but it is strongly recommended that all persons interested in further study of juvenile crime read the original article.

In reviewing the developmental research work of McCord and McCord, Sears, Maccoby and Levin, Adorno, Frenkel-Brunswik, and Levinson on the effects of discipline, Shore concluded: "These findings are consistent with experimental studies of punishment. Punishment is effective in bringing about short term conformity, but does not lead to internalization of moral values or behavioral controls useful in other situations over long periods of time." Shore further stated that the induction methods of explanations and withdrawal of affection are more effective in producing internalized controls than sensitization techniques of verbal and physical attacks which make a child anticipate punishment from an external source.

In reviewing developmental research on social learning in criminal behavior, Shore discussed Bandura and Walters' theory that: "The violence to which a child is exposed during the period of his growth when imitation and identification are important cause him to model himself after the aggressor." In this connection, Shore noted Kohlberg's description of two types of identification: personal and positional. The former, involving close emotional ties and a wish to be like the parent, is related to moral learning through the capacity for empathy and guilt. In contrast, positional identification involves a wish to usurp the parent's power role and is not related to moral learning.

In his review of psychodynamic theories of criminal behavior, Shore cited Johnson and Szurek's work on "how parents can unconsciously gain satisfaction from their child's antisocial behavior that they subtly provoke and perpetuate." Shore also referred to Erikson's concept of a "negative [against society] identity" which for many is a defense against "no identity."

In his review of social psychological theories related to criminal behavior, Shore outlined the research findings of Reckless, Dinitz and Murray, Bandura and Walters, and Massimo and Shore, which indicate that individuals with low self-esteem are more susceptible to pressures toward delinquent behavior than individuals with adequate self-esteem.

Shore concluded his review of the literature with the following observation: "No single factor has yet been found to be most decisive in preventing crime. Any program for crime prevention must be comprehensive and multidimensional."

Testing of Specific Theories of Causation

The most promising new research on the subject of juvenile delinquency involves the proposing and testing of specific theories of causation.

In his 1976 article, "Investigating the Interrelations Among Social Control Variables and Conformity," Rankin discusses the new control theories and tests some of their hypotheses. According to control theorists, everyone experiences pressure or motivation to deviate. Therefore, what is needed is an explanation of conformity. Control theorists reason that the weaker the individual's commitment to the common value system of society, the greater the probability of delinquent activity.

Rankin indicated that one control theorist, Reckless, predicted that inner containment is more important than outer containment in controlling crime. Inner containment is measured by such variables as educational expectations, attitude toward the law, and attachment to school. Outer containment is measured by such variables as number of delinquent companions (the greater the number, the less the containment) and participation in conventional activities. Rankin's research (1976) failed to support Reckless's hypothesis. The number of delinquent companions was found to be the strongest factor in predicting delinquent behavior.

Another control theorist, Hirschi, predicted that high stakes in conformity are associated with lower delinquency. Rankin (1976) found this to be true when the adolescent had no delinquent friends, but the opposite was true for adolescents with delinquent companions. Evidently, a high need for conformity can lead to either prosocial or antisocial behavior, depending upon the group with whom the individual is associating.

In his 1976 article, "Testing Alternative Models of Delinquent Causation," Hepburn schematically contrasted the causation theories of Sutherland, Glueck, and Hirschi as in the figures on pages 16 and 17.

Hepburn's research data (1976) supported Hirschi's model more often than the other two models and Glueck's model more often than Sutherland's. Moreover, the following revised Hirschi model gained even greater support, although not to the complete exclusion of the other two models.

In contrast to Rankin's findings that point to the significance of number of delinquent friends as a predictor of delinquent behavior, these data point to lack of family support as the strongest predictive factor in delinquent behavior. Rankin (1976) depicted Hirschi's explanation of the significance of lack of family support as follows: "Lack of attachment to parents is directly conducive to delinquency because the unattached child does not have to consider consequences of his actions for his relationship with his parents."

Figure 1.

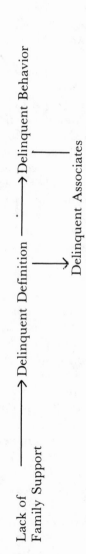

*Self-definition as a delinquent.

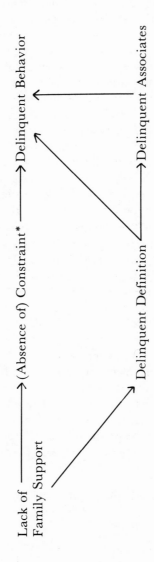

Figure 2.

Revised Hirschi Model

*External controls on behavior.

Comparison of Structural Theories and Control Theories

Cernkovich (1978b) pointed out that the structural theory of the genesis of delinquency is usualy applied to lower-class delinquency. According to this theory the individual's socio-economic position in society is the crucial variable in delinquency: "Structural based pressures more or less drive the individual into delinquency as an adaptation or reaction." On the other hand, the control theory which explains delinquency in terms of weakened or broken ties to the conventional normative order is usually applied to middle-class delinquency. In his article, "Value Orientations and Delinquency Involvement" (1978a), Cernkovich reported findings that do not support the assumption that delinquency is class linked. Delinquency involvement was found to evidence a significant negative association with conventional value orientations and this relationship was found to persist in all socioeconomic strata.

Later on (1978b) Cernkovich tested the predictive utility of both the structural and control models across a wide range of social status positions. Analysis of the data indicates that both models accounted for significant though small proportions of the variance in delinquent involvement. The control model accounted for significantly more variance in delinquency (12.6%) than did the structural model (8%), and the major component of the structural variance was the level of perceived opportunity (7.5%) in contrast to only .5% for socioeconomic status. When variables from both models were included in a single regression equation, the amount of variance increased to 14.5%. Cernkovich concluded: "The effect of socio-economic status on delinquency involvement is largely indirect through its influence on perceptions of limited opportunities and value orientations. Perceptions of limited opportunities affects delinquency largely through its impact on value orientations."

Effects of Various Treatment and Rehabilitation Methods

In their 1935 book, *Roots of Crime*, psychoanalysts Alexander and Healy made an observation whose truth has been noted over and over since then. "All who have studied large numbers of offenders know very many cases in which punishment does not check criminal tendencies.... Punishment occasionally appears even to be sought."

After surveying different methods employed to prevent future delinquencies, Dudycha (1955) argued for psychological treatment of juvenile delinquents. He pointed out that restraint has been used for centuries and crime still flourishes. Evidently, restraint does not reach the disease, just the symptom. Improvement of physical conditions also does not strike at the heart of the problem, i.e., what motivates delinquent behavior. Similarly, organized recreation does not prevent delinquency because in many cases delinquency arises from frustrations in the home. It was Dudycha's opinion that psychological approaches in the form of counseling, guidance, and parent education with its emphasis on the individual gets at the crux of the child's problems.

Many clinicians have discovered that traditional psychotherapy which emphasizes understanding of the causes of behavior is often not effective in treating delinquents. In his book, *Reality Therapy* (1965), Glasser presented a new method for treating delinquents that has been adopted by many other clinicians in their work with acting-out individuals. This method emphasizes the necessity for individuals to take responsibility for their behavior instead of hiding behind the excuse of past suffering.

In their book, *The Criminal Personality* (1977), Yochelson and Samenow described their treatment approach which differs from traditional therapies and resembles Glasser's reality therapy. Instead of delving into past traumas that might have led to criminal behavior, Yochelson and Samenow focus on errors in the criminals' thinking that encourage them to act out in ways which hurt both themselves and others.

In their article, "Confrontation of Self Through Outdoor Challenge: Pennsylvania's Outdoor Experience for Juvenile Offenders" (1976), Brown and Simpson indicated that a six-week rigorous outdoor program utilized as an alternative to traditional programs was effective in providing self-confrontation, enhancing self-concept, and developing understanding of others and respect for them. From what we know about causation of delinquency, these changes would reduce the likelihood of delinquent behavior.

Another innovative approach, recently aired on television, was the rehabilitative program called "Scared Straight," in which juvenile delinquents are brought into a prison to hear the convicts describe the misery of prison life. The experience reportedly moves even the toughest delinquents to abruptly stop their delinquent behavior. However, recent reports indicate that the success of this method is greatly exaggerated and in some situations it is actually related to a higher rate of recidivism than no treatment. Obviously, more research is needed to determine the specific set of circumstances in which this program is effective in deterring delinquency.

SUMMARY

This review of the literature points to several important conclusions:

1. Juvenile delinquency is a multifaceted, multidetermined phenomenon requiring a multidimensional approach to treatment and prevention.
2. The majority of juvenile offenders limit their activities to minor offenses. Only a minority of juvenile offenders are dangerous.
3. Most juvenile offenders outgrow their delinquencies.
4. Factors associated with high rates of delinquency, ranging from the general to the specific, include: opportunities perceived as limited due to low socioeconomic status; delinquent associates and peer-group pressure; problems in the home, including instability, violence, inadequate nurturance, and overly rigid or overly permissive discipline; weak ties to conventional values; low self-esteem and low self-confidence; inborn or environmental handicaps to development.
5. Lack of close family ties appears to be the primary factor in most cases of delinquency.
6. Methods of discipline emphasizing internal controls (guilt, empathy) are more effective than those emphasizing external controls (fear of punishment).

7. Some families encourage delinquent behavior.
8. Some delinquents relish punishment.
9. In many cases, psychological treatment emphasizing individual responsibility and consequences of behavior is more effective at controlling delinquent behavior than treatment aimed at developing insight into causes of behavior.

Chapter 2

SIGNIFICANCE OF SCHOOL ADJUSTMENT

The importance of a good school adjustment in preventing juvenile delinquency cannot be overemphasized. Behavioral maladjustment in school and learning disabilities have long been associated with delinquency. In addition, researchers in the field of delinquency regard a negative attitude toward school as a sign of a low stake in conventional society and a strong element juvenile delinquency. Friday and Halsey (1977) reported: "When parents have poor attitudes toward school and the importance of achieving, there is a higher probability that their children will be delinquent." Cohen (1955) argued that the delinquent gang permits working-class boys to recoup self-esteem lost through defeat in middle-class institutions, such as school.

Research shows that low verbal IQs and poor reading are strongly related to delinquency (Andrew 1979). In other words, the weaker the ability to express oneself verbally, the greater the chance of acting-out behavior. In a study to determine whether poor reading also relates to the seriousness as well as

22

the incidence of delinquency, Andrew (1979) compared the violence records of good vs. poor readers. Andrew proposed that, "the level of verbal ability may not be as important in the regulation of behavior as is the (usually related) readiness to learn to the extent of one's capability." An achievement quotient was obtained for each subject based on the difference between their Wechsler Verbal IQs and their Wide Range Achievement Test Reading IQ-type standard scores. The results of the study supported the hypothesized link between poor reading achievement quotients and high violence histories.

In my clinical experience, I have repeatedly observed that school is the first place the future delinquent's behavior deteriorates. The youngster cannot keep up with the work or loses interest in it. His or her low school achievement reduces self-esteem. Then the "ditching" begins. Idle and unsupervised for long periods of time, the juvenile starts experimenting more and more with drugs and minor delinquent acts. Before long juveniles find themselves involved in more and more serious delinquencies which a short time earlier they would have shunned.

Creating or restoring the juvenile offender's interest in school is a crucial aspect of rehabilitation, particularly if the juvenile is too young to obtain regular employment. Furthermore, it is my clinical impression that one of the best prognostic indicators of whether reformed delinquents will stay out of trouble is how well they sustain their newly developed interest in school after leaving a rehabilitation program.

It is obvious that early detection and treatment of school problems is one of the major tools we have to prevent the later development of delinquent behavior.

Chapter 3

ISSUES IN DECIDING APPROPRIATE TREATMENT AND PLACEMENT OF JUVENILE OFFENDERS

The major controversy in the treatment of juvenile offenders is the effectiveness of punishment. Laboratory research with animals has demonstrated that punishment does not permanently eradicate undesired behavior, but merely suppresses such behavior for a period of time. Laboratory research goes on to show that the only way to completely eliminate undesired behavior is to reinforce alternate behavior. Of course, punishment may work to eliminate undesired behavior by suppressing it long enough to permit the learning of new, more acceptable behavior that will, with proper reinforcement, completely replace the undesired behavior.

Many people in the juvenile justice system are convinced that, in order to diminish the likelihood of future offenses, all juvenile offenders must face some negative consequence of their acting-out behavior. Many clinicians, particularly those in agreement with the principles of reality therapy, would support this idea. But then there is the question of what negative consequence is advisable. In some cases a planned punishment is not even needed: a police contact may be sufficient to prevent any future law violations. In other cases, years of incarceration seem to have little or no effect.

Moreover, many observers in the field are convinced that what is ordinarily viewed as punishment by most is actually rewarding to some. These observations lead to the conclusion that the issue of punishment should be dealt with on an individual basis.

On the other hand, the proponents of fixed or determinant sentencing according to the crime argue that punishment affects not only the offender who is being punished, but also every would-be offender. They believe that the definite knowledge of the punishment for a particular crime is the best deterrent to that crime. In other words, certainty of punishment is even more important than amount of punishment.

While recognizing the logic in the arguments for fixed sentencing, my experience counseling juvenile offenders leads me to disagree. It appears that most juvenile offenders avoid anxiety about the consequences of their behavior by believing they will not be caught or by pushing out of their minds what consequences they will have to face if they are caught. In other cases where there is greater awareness of the risk of being caught and punished, this knowledge seems to heighten the excitement of the criminal activity and the satisfaction of getting away with it. Moreover, these observations seem to hold true even in situations where the risk is extremely high (for example, when the juvenile, having already received a suspended sentence, knows that getting caught for a new offense would mean incarceration).

Evidently, individuals prone to criminal behavior do not think the way other people think. They do not take cause and effect relationships into consideration the way most people do; knowledge of consequences does not affect them the way proponents of fixed sentencing suppose. But this should not be surprising. Offenders would not have entertained thoughts of criminal activities in the first place if they had been thinking like other people. Incidentally, this is precisely the main point of Yochelson and Samenow's book, *The Criminal Personality*.

Another reason for my opposition to fixed sentencing is my philosophy that punishment should be no greater than needed to effect a change in behavior. In other words, rehabilitation rather than vengeance should be the purpose of punishment. Moreover, if there is any way other than punishment to change behavior, it is preferable because punishment does not guarantee long-lasting change. This philosophy leads to the main thesis of this book, i.e., decisions about punishment and treatment of offenders should be based on the individual committing the crime, rather than on the crime itself. As for the protection of society, in my opinion this approach offers much more protection to society than fixed sentencing. There is much greater risk of repeated offenses from someone who has paid for a past crime by a period of incarceration than from someone who has been helped to overcome whatever problems led to the criminal behavior.

In considering the appropriate treatment and placement of a juvenile offender, several questions must be asked. First, is confinement in a secure facility for the protection of society necessary? If the offender is not a serious threat to society, the next question that arises is whether the individual can be rehabilitated while living at home. Is the individual's behavior so out of control or is he or she so emotionally disturbed as to require placement in a rehabilitation or treatment facility? On the other hand, are the problems in the family so great that it is advisable to make a placement with relatives or in a foster home?

If it is decided that the offender can remain at home, is supervision by the probation officer sufficient to prevent future offenses? Should the offender be enrolled in some sort of work, educational, or recreational program? Should the offender receive counseling or therapy, individually or with his or her family? Should treatment be primarily confrontive to underscore individual responsibility, supportive to build self-esteem, probing to develop insight, or oriented to practical issues to improve coping mechanisms?

All these questions are considered in the treatment recommendations for different types of juvenile offenders described in Chapters 5 through 14.

Chapter 4

TYPICAL DELINQUENTS

The first group that we will consider are the so-called "typical" delinquents. These are the juvenile offenders whose psychiatric and psychological examinations reveal no significant psychological problems. In other words, they do not show signs of being either seriously emotionally disturbed or arrested at an early stage of psychological development. Their deviance lies in their values, rather than their psychological makeup. For one reason or another, they have rejected the values of society at large and instead have adopted the values of a socially deviant subgroup. In most, but not all, instances these delinquents live in underprivileged neighborhoods where gangs prevail and crime is common. While this often helps to explain the development of delinquency within the individual, it is not the full explanation. Usually the families also play an important role.

In some cases, parents have been models of irresponsibility, either blatantly or subtly. In the former situation, children repeatedly see and hear their parents go against society's rules. In the most extreme examples, the parents actually involve their children in crimes whenever small size or young age is an asset. It is easy to understand how children growing up in this atmosphere will have little if any conflict about engaging in illegal activities.

In the more subtle situation of a parent saying one thing and doing another, the child will eventually see through the hypocrisy and ignore what the parent says. This situation was vividly demonstrated in counseling with one family. The father repeatedly expressed shock at his son's stealing cars for the purpose of joyriding. The father would stress over and over that there had never been a thief before in his entire family. Nevertheless, when his son stole some sneakers and other things he needed for school, his father let him keep them. It was pointed out that in permitting his son to keep the stolen merchandise he was saving himself the money the items would have cost, and he was in effect an accessory to the crime. The father responded to this by blandly stating that if it ever happened again he would make his son return whatever he stole. In another example, a 15-year-old girl charged with several armed robberies indicated she had committed several prior offenses and all her mother did was warn her about the consequences. "My mother tells me not to do something. 'You'll get in trouble. Just wait until you get in trouble.'... I never got punished in my whole life. My mom never punishes with restrictions. That's stupid. We never heard of that in my family."

In some cases, the parents set an example of responsibility and respectability, but failed to instill their values in their children. In these situations it appears that the parents were so caught up in their own lives that they were not truly available to give their children the love and attention they needed. As a result, their children turned to other persons to fill the void and serve as models of behavior, and the delinquent peer group stepped in as parent substitutes.

In high-delinquency areas there are cases where the blame seems to lie more with the neighborhood than with the families. It appears that these families would have done an adequate job socializing their youngsters in a neighborhood where there was more support for their values. As it is, only the strongest families in high-delinquency areas are able to offset the powerful influence of the prevalent delinquent subculture.

Two examples come to mind. In the first, a 13½-year-old boy charged with a series of strong-armed robberies described the influence of his delinquent peers as follows: "I want to be good, but when I get with some of my friends...they want to do something. They tell me they did it before and made money. So I do it to have some money like them." Psychological testing indicated that this boy was fully capable of delaying his impulses and thinking ahead to consequences. On the other hand, testing indicated that irresponsible, antisocial behavior was so common in his experience that he accepted it as a norm. Lacking any clear idea of right and wrong, he joined his friends in whatever fun or profitable activity he thought he could get away with.

In another case, a 17-year-old boy was in trouble with the law for the first time because he severely beat someone who offended him. His experience of being poor all his life, living in neighborhoods full of violence and crime, filled him with determination to make a better life for himself. He worked hard to improve himself and he had already obtained a job with a promising future. Despite the advances he had made, his psychological test data were filled with themes of predation, violence, and stealing. Apparently, his frequent exposure to antisocial behavior made him see it more or less as a norm and, although he was striving to be better than the delinquents in his neighborhood, he was not totally adverse to resorting to their tactics when he felt a particular need to do so.

Treatment

In considering what measures should be taken to combat juvenile crime due to a rejection of society's values, it is obvious that steps should be taken to decrease antisocial attitudes. As long as an individual is underprivileged, he or she has no real stake in society, no reason to accept society's values. Thus, large-scale improvement of social and economic conditions in deprived neighborhoods is one way of fighting juvenile delinquency. Specific measures that can be used to improve an individual delinquent's stake in society include: tutoring to enhance school performance, job training and placement, and participation in activities that are both enjoyable and character building.

While these positive measures are greatly preferred to punishment because they are aimed at treating causes rather than symptoms, they are not always sufficient to stop delinquent activity. In some cases it is necessary to resort to punishment in the form of a work assignment or loss of freedom in an effort to make the criminal activity less appealing. While the punishment will not totally eradicate the criminal tendencies, it may suppress the criminal activity long enough for the individual to find rewards in more socially acceptable behavior.

Chapter 5

IDENTITY PROBLEMS

More than at any other time in life, adolescence is a time of looking at one's self to discover who one really is. In this search for one's identity, it is common to try on different roles to see how they fit. An adolescent may idolize a celebrity, an older friend, or a popular peer and consciously or unconsciously try to be as much like that person as possible. Sometimes a group phenomenon occurs whereby everybody in the group tries to measure up to the group ideal of "coolness," or "toughness," or "badness." Some cases of identity problems precipitate criminal behavior.

Doubts About Masculinity

A common example of criminal behavior from identity problems is the teenage boy who overcompensates for his doubts about his masculinity by adopting a tough macho image and engaging in criminal activity to "prove" to himself and others that he is a "real" man.

In one such case, a 13-year-old boy, arrested for the first time for a strong-armed robbery, swaggered into the psychologist's office with an air of bravado and belligerently stated: "I hate psychiatrists. I got rooked into this." When asked about his apparent accent, he indicated he was imitating the way they talk in gangster movies because, "I want to be a gangster." When it was suggested to him that in that event, he will probably be locked up a lot, he said: "No, I'll be broken out." Then he volunteered, "I also want to be a cop." He indicated that he thought it would make him a better cop to first learn about a life of crime. When it was suggested that he probably could not get hired as a policeman if he has a serious criminal record, he acknowledged that in that case, he better stop his criminal activities. As the interview moved on to a discussion of his favorite TV programs, this boy's belligerence receded even further and he became very engaging and friendly. When the psychologist commented that he was much more likeable this way and asked why he puts on such a tough act, he said: "It's the people I hang around with. I get the impression of them and I act like them. I don't want to hang around with them fairies [other kids]. The kids I hang around with go to the canyon. They cuss the teachers. The others, the goody-goody fairies do something behind your back." Although this boy experimented with criminal behavior in a misguided effort to prove his masculinity, the test data indicated that his basic ideals and values were far from antisocial. His choice of three wishes were as follows: "Stop crime. Wish for all peace, no fighting at all. Everybody would just be happy."

Another case of an overly tough exterior to cover up feelings of vulnerability and doubts about masculinity involved a mildly delinquent 16-year old boy who was removed from his foster home because of some aggressive comments he had made. This boy indicated that he liked living in the foster home and was sorry he could not stay. "We got in a big hassle. I was telling them how I felt. The next day the counselor took me out." He related how he unwittingly hurt one of the children's feelings by something he had said. It bothered him so much, he told his foster parents, "I could hurt somebody and not even mean to." He explained to the psychologist, "I didn't mean boom boom. I just meant emotionally." He also warned his foster parents that if his foster father ever tried to hit him, he would not take it. He would fight back. Upon questioning, he admitted the foster father had never actually threatened him. However, he had noticed how big and strong his foster father was and he decided that the foster father could really mess him over if he wanted to. In this context, the boy said: "If I lose a fight, I don't whine and lick my wounds and wait for someone to pick me up. I pick myself up and say, 'You want to go another round.'...You've got to be tough to survive." After reviewing this boy's projective test responses, the psychologist told this boy that he was not really a violent person, he just had a big mouth that made him sound violent. This boy responded to these words (which the psychologist had not intended to be taken negatively) as if he had been struck. His eyes filled with tears, he turned his head away, and he accused the psychologist of calling him a girl (which he expressed in crude, descriptive terms). He also threatened to walk out of the interview if that was what the psychologist meant. Only after much reassurance that all that was meant was that he was not a dangerous person did the boy calm down and turn to face the psychologist again.

In some instances a tough exterior is not intended to cover up doubts about masculinity as much as it is an attempt to camouflage sensitive feelings which are regarded as a sign of weakness. In one such case, an angry, belligerent 15-year-old boy presented himself as a super-independent, super-confident, antisocial individual. He attributed his rage to the wrongs of society which he expounded upon at great length. However, it seemed more likely, despite his denials, that his real anger was with his parents for not providing him with a home in which he could really feel at home. His mother left him and his younger siblings with his father when he was a young child. Years later during a conflict with his father and step-mother, his father abruptly informed him that he was not his real father. Soon afterwards this boy decided to live with his mother whom he did not know well and who could not by herself replace the family life to which he had been accustomed. Psychological testing confirmed the clinical impression of a deep sense of hurt in this boy beneath his air of bravado. Sev-

eral of his Rorschach responses reflected feelings of victimiza-
tion and the outstretched arms in his human figure drawings
seemed to represent a reaching out for help.

Not all teenage boys with doubts about their masculinity
adopt an air of bravado. Some appear as passive as they feel.
They might become preoccupied with guns as a representation
of their masculine strivings. For example, a 13-year-old boy
raised in an all-female environment had been a behavior problem for years. While a runaway from a residential treatment
facility he broke into a house to take some food. He noticed a
rifle and took it because, "I wanted to shoot it. I like guns."
"Did you want to shoot it at anybody?" he was asked. "No
way. I just like shooting at targets," he responded. Psychological testing showed him to be an anxious, insecure, basically
passive individual despite many psychological strengths. The
test data also suggested that at times he tried to overcome his
feelings of weakness and vulnerability by exaggerated asser-
tions of masculine strength and activity. In all likelihood, his
fascination with guns served this function. One of his TAT
(Thematic Apperception Test) stories clearly depicted his
strong need for this symbolic expression of masculinity to
compensate for his feelings of weakness and inadequacy. "This
kid's gun is broken and he's crying about it."

Some passive males dream of acquiring a fast car or
motorcycle to boost their masculine self-image. When the possibility of acquiring one seems remote, some boys resort to
theft. In one such case, a slightly built, soft spoken, gently
mannered, sad looking 16-year-old high school dropout was
arrested for stealing a motorcycle. Psychological testing showed
him to be an overly inhibited individual, weighed down by feelings of sadness, weakness, and inadequacy. In an apparent
effort to overcome these feelings, he developed a strong ambition to accomplish something great, to really be someone.
However, it appeared that he had not yet figured out how to
achieve this. His intense yearning for a motorcycle seemed to
reflect a magical belief that a motorcycle would supply him
with the strength and power he felt he was lacking.

Doubts About Femininity

While the establishment of a secure male identity seems to be much more of an issue in our society than the establishment of a secure female identity, this does not mean that females are without problems in their sexual identities. Whereas males feel pressured to be strong and powerful, females feel pressured to be physically attractive and popular with the opposite sex. Furthermore, though males exhibit a much higher rate of acting-out behavior to "prove" their masculinity, acting-out behavior also occurs among females to "prove" their femininity.

One 15½-year-old girl who was referred for a psychological evaluation because of her beyond-control behavior, including runaways and alcohol usage, eloquently expressed her disillusionment with her social life. "Every time I have a boyfriend, he always seems to drop me for someone else. I feel there is an imaginary line of dudes and I'm passed on from one to another." She further confided that one of her boyfriends treated her very badly even when they were going together. Though average in appearance, this girl expressed great dissatisfaction with the way she looked and a strong conviction that her appearance put her in a weak bargaining position for popularity. Apparently, she had been using sex in an effort to affirm her worth as a female, only to have the opposite effect. Psychological testing further demonstrated this girl's high-level perceptions coupled with her intense need for peer, particularly male, acceptance and her neurotic conflicts about this need. Themes of clinging dependency and disappointment in others pervaded her TAT. For example, in response to one picture she said: "That's me trying to hang onto somebody and he's slowly slipping away." In response to a picture which usually elicits themes of personal ambition or parental pressures toward achievement, she gave the following story: "At first he wanted to get in the band. He wanted to be part of the gang. All the people he wanted to hang out with were part of the band. Then he found out they weren't the kind of people he wanted to hang around with so he kind of gave up." Though this girl wanted to overcome her extreme dependency on others, it was evident from the following Rorschach response that she was very torn between her need for peer approval and her awareness of what is right. "Looks like two faces. Like one side's telling what you should do and the other side's telling you something different, like your conscience."

Conflict Between Being Good or Bad

Some juveniles, feeling they can never measure up to what adults expect of them, give up the effort to be "good" with a certain sense of relief and adopt the opposite role of being "bad." Several case examples come to mind. In the first, a 17-year-old boy became mildly delinquent when he gave up the role of being an ideal son and rebelled against his mother's extreme restrictions on his behavior because he decided that the rewards of being his mother's favorite child were not enough to compensate for what he felt he was missing as a regular teenager.

In a similar case, a 16-year-old boy who had been a model student and son decided to join his younger brother in delinquent activities when he got tired of always being the good one in the family without sufficient recognition and appreciation from his parents.

In the case of a 14-year-old boy charged with several burglaries, psychological testing revealed a deep sense of inadequacy despite evidence of many strengths. He seemed to have a feeling that he was absolutely "good for nothing." In the interview he indicated that he interpreted the teachings of his fundamentalist religion to mean that he was doomed, so he might as well keep doing bad things. He also took a teacher's comment about the stupidity of getting into a lot of trouble for stealing little things as an inspiration to steal big things.

In another case, a Black, 17-year-old high school senior had been very success-oriented prior to a sudden rash of criminal behavior which he could not explain. "I don't know. I hope I won't [do it again], but I don't know. I lose control and I do things I ordinarily wouldn't do....I wasn't myself." His upwardly mobile parents raised him to ignore the issue of race and to believe there were no limits to what he could do. As a result, he couldn't understand why his white girlfriend's father tried to break up their relationship. "I never did anything to him." He could not grasp the fact of racial prejudice. Suffering greatly from what he felt to be a total repudiation of himself and all the positive things he had accomplished, this boy engaged in criminal activities in an apparent effort to prove he was as worthless as he believed his girlfriend's father considered him.

Conflicts About Growing Up

For some teenagers the identity crisis revolves primarily around conflicts about growing up, particularly the issues of dependency vs. autonomy.

A 15-year-old girl got involved in overly grown-up behavior, yet on confinement she related to others in a very immature manner. Psychological testing revealed that though she had the potential to behave in a mature manner, she had deep conflicts about growing up. She was striving to achieve independence from a dominating mother figure. At the same time, she yearned to return to an idealized image of a satisfying childhood. In addition, she was torn between expressing her aggressive and sexual impulses, on the one hand, and her desire to remain a pure, angelic little girl, on the other. She was also very concerned about what kind of person she would grow up to be and what kind of role she would fill in the future.

In another case, a 17-year-old girl referred for a psychological evaluation because of her beyond-control, explosive behavior presented herself as a breezily confident, independent individual. However, she had not managed to make much progress toward her extremely high goals because of such behavior as dropping out of school and not working at a steady job to earn the money she needed for the specialized training she desired. Psychological testing revealed much underlying depression related to frustrated needs for nurturance. Beneath this girl's outwardly independent air were deep-seated dependency needs, and she would never achieve her goals until she resolved the conflict between these contradictory forces in her personality.

Problems Related to Being Adopted

Many adopted children have a particularly tumultuous adolescence after a relatively peaceful, well-adjusted childhood. It seems that for them the issues of identity are greatly magnified. They are concerned not only with what kind of persons they are going to be, but also where they really belong and what their natural parents were like. Their problems are compounded when they begin to act out to test their adoptive parent's commitment to them. Unfortunately, some adoptive parents, reacting to the dramatic transformation of their sweet child into a belligerent teenager, begin to have some misgivings about the adoption, which the supersensitive adopted teenager manages to detect. Naturally, this only increases the adopted child's sense of not really belonging in the adoptive family. In one case the issue was made quite blatant when the adoptive father told his daughter, in a fit of rage, that adopting her was the biggest mistake of his life.

Problems About Being Different

Anything that sets a teenager apart from peers adds fuel to the typical adolescent identity crisis. Since a major task of adolescence and a major step in identity formation is to establish independence from one's family, peer acceptance assumes greater significance then than at any other time in life. In the process of breaking away from one's family en route to establishing independent identity, adolescents go through a stage of excessive dependency on peer approval. Thus, adolescents willingly conform to rigid standards set by peers at the very same time they are "proving" their independence by resisting adult authority. Anything interfering with the adolescent's acceptance by the peer group is extremely painful to him or her and may prompt acting-out behavior.

A 14-year-old girl of white and black parentage was referred for a psychological evaluation because of her explosive, beyond-control behavior. In response to a question about how she gets along with other kids, she confided the social discomfort she experienced as a result of her mixed racial background. "I get along with everybody. I'm not prejudiced against any color, but they might be prejudiced against me. Some of the white girls are stuck up to me. They act like 'Miss Know-it-all.'...The Blacks consider me white. The whites consider me Black. They don't recognize that I'm half white...I consider myself half and half." According to her mother this girl had had no social or behavior problems until her teens. Psychological testing confirmed that she was capable of a high level of functioning. Although this girl was also troubled by a lack of a positive relationship with a father or father substitute, it was evident that problems in her social identity was a major factor in her behavior problems.

A 15-year-old boy with several moderately disabling birth defects was referred for a psychological evaluation following his arrest for trespassing while a runaway. When questioned as to why he ran away from his grandparents' home, he related incident after incident of what he felt was his grandfather putting him down because of his physical problems. He himself minimized their negative effect. "It does not bother me. I can do stuff." He said he could run and play sports well and, whenever he has been prevented from participating in sports, he has done such things as write a sports newspaper. As for his peers teasing him, the boy said that kids who have confidence in themselves accept him for what he is; only kids who lack self-confidence tease him, and he ignores them. While all this appeared to represent a very healthy adaptation to his physical defects, his social history indicated that his tendency to minimize their impact had caused him to be lax in his care of one defect and to sabotage treatment of another. In addition, there were other indications that he was not as adapted to his physical problems as he tried to appear. For one thing, he said he would kill himself if there was anything more wrong with him. For another, he expressed great concern throughout the interview and testing about how he may appear to others and whether they might think he was nuts or had something wrong with him. It appeared that his excessive concern with people's opinions of his psychological intactness was a displacement of his anxiety about their opinions of his physical defects. Third, this boy said his grandfather claimed that he buys friendships by giving his friends money and things. He denied this, but it was apparent from various comments he made that he was willing to forgive a great deal of inconsideration on the part of his friends as long as they continued to be his friends. It seemed likely that this boy felt in a weak position socially because of his physical defects and, as a result, was willing to put up with more, and give more, than is usual in order to maintain his friendships.

Treatment

It is obvious that punishment is not the solution to acting-out behavior stemming from identity problems. Therapy is needed in these cases to help the individual find constructive ways of working through identity problems. In addition, activities that encourage positive identities are also desirable, e.g., survival training in the wilderness for boys who feel the need to prove their masculinity.

When therapy and other positive measures fail to stop the acting-out behavior, punishment might suppress the acting-out behavior long enough to enable the individual to develop more socially acceptable behavior. However, in some cases punishment actually feeds the problem. A 15-year-old boy commented that prior to coming to juvenile hall he had been afraid, but he had discovered he could handle it. Then he was afraid of the county rehabilitation center, but he learned he could handle that too. Now he was afraid of the state youth prison, but he sort of looked on that as a challenge to see if he could handle that too. Evidently, this boy regarded increasing punishment as something akin to a primitive puberty rite whereby he could prove his manhood.

Chapter 6

SUDDEN BREAKDOWN OF RIGID CONTROLS

There are some juvenile offenders whose unlawful activity is a shock to everybody who knows them. They are usually very well behaved and they are among the last to be suspected of serious wrongdoing. Psychological evaluations reveal that their characteristically good behavior is maintained at a heavy cost. They rigidly suppress their angry impulses while tension builds up inside them. Then something happens (the proverbial "straw that breaks the camel's back") to break their tight controls and these normally inhibited individuals suddenly become overly aggressive. The form their aggression takes depends upon such factors as fear of consequences and level of conscience development. In noncriminal cases the aggression is strictly verbal, while criminal cases involve physical aggression against property or persons. In some instances, the aggression is expressed directly at the object of the individual's anger. In others it is displaced to an object that the individual perceives as less likely to retaliate.

Often the tremendous anger that the individual had been suppressing prior to the offense is related to family conflict. For example, a 14-year-old boy and a companion entered what they thought to be an abandoned house and did $15,000 worth of damage to the interior, including destruction of walls, ceilings, and furnishings. This boy gave no reason for his actions except that he was angry with his parents because they would not let him quit his paper route. His parents said this behavior was totally out of character for him. They described him as basically very well behaved though somewhat irresponsible in doing his homework and completing tasks. He had wanted to quit his afternoon paper route during the summer because he believed it would prevent him from going to the beach with his friends. He carefully explained this to his parents, but they were adamant. They had decided it was time he behaved responsibly and they were going to make sure he did. Powerless to change their minds and afraid to let them know the intensity of his rage, he let it out in a way he mistakenly thought would have no repercussions. Psychological testing indicated that this boy was an emotionally blocked individual who tended to deny and rationalize away unpleasant situations rather than deal with them and whose ambivalence about almost everything prevented him from utilizing his considerable inner resources to achieve his rather high goals.

In another case, a sad looking 17-year-old boy was referred for a psychological evaluation following his arrest for malicious mischief involving the destruction of property in a trailer court. Speaking slowly in a low voice, his whole manner bespoke passivity and defeat. He indicated that he had been drunk the night he committed his crime. Psychological testing revealed marked inhibition of feelings coupled with marked repression of inner thoughts. It was as if he had put himself into a box so he would not have any trouble with the outside world and then had put blinders in his mind so he would not be upset by anything going on inside his head. He was apparently using alcohol to lift his neurotic inhibitions but went too far in loosening his normally tight controls.

In still another case of indirect aggression, a 15-year-old boy was arrested for joining a friend in an attempt to set fire to an office in his high school. His parents expressed great surprise on learning of his actions because he was normally very well behaved. They indicated that he was very helpful around the house and he never used bad language. Psychological testing showed him to have a lot of sad feelings locked inside. In addition, he appeared to be a somewhat immature individual who had difficulty understanding and handling complicated social situations. However, there were no indications of impulsive acting-out or violent tendencies. In the interview he expressed a great deal of discomfort over his sick grandmother's temporary presence in his home. "We don't have any homelife anymore. We can't talk as loud as we used to. We don't invite friends over anymore." He also stated that his grandmother took over his bedroom while he slept on the floor of his sister's room. Moreover, his grandmother pulled down all his posters of nature scenes and was asking for his room to be painted a color he despised. He believed there was nothing he could do about the situation so he tried to go along with it. In another context, he mentioned that he does not like to make "waves" so he "avoids hassles." Apparently, he acted out in an effort to relieve the tension that was building up inside him.

A 15½-year-old boy referred for a psychological evaluation after physically assaulting two older women in attempts to snatch their purses appeared extremely tense. Although he kept his emotions tightly in check, he looked as if he was ready to "jump out of his skin" at any moment. He indicated he would have preferred a male psychologist to do the evaluation because of his nervousness with older people and the opposite sex. Considering his history, this boy's uneasiness with women was not at all surprising. He lived with his mother following his parents' divorce, but when he was nine his mother sent him to live with his father because neighbors blamed him for some damage to their property. He denied any anger toward his mother, even though he claimed he was not the one responsible for the property damage. He said he had no feeling about his mother, "because I haven't been with her for years." This boy hated his first stepmother. "She was a bitch. She didn't like me." She threw this boy and his father out five or six times and finally got a divorce. Then this boy and his father went to live with his grandmother. At first it was "all right," but then there were problems and he and his father had to move elsewhere. The father then married a woman this boy liked, but soon they were divorced. This boy explained his purse snatching in terms of his wanting money for pot. "I always feel tense, except when I am by myself or unless I am stoned.... I thought it was the easiest way to get money without hurting anyone. I heard one of them fall. I didn't feel so good after that." Psychological testing showed this boy to be extremely constricted in his inner feelings and in his reactions to external stimuli. His imagination seemed to serve as an outlet for his bottled up feelings, but only partially. At times his imagination was very alive, but often it was inactive. Like his sketchy, substanceless human figure drawings, it appeared that this boy was going through life in the shadow of existence without ever fully participating. Although he had an interest in close relationships, he had difficulty feeling close to anyone, and particular difficulty relating to females on even a superficial basis. It seemed likely that his long history of unhappy relationships with women entered into his decision to steal money in the manner he did. Symbolically, it was as if he was trying to snatch from women the nurturance he felt women never gave him voluntarily. There was no evidence in the interview or test data of strong aggressive impulses.

In a tragic case involving direct aggression, a 15-year-old girl who was normally extremely well behaved acted out her long built-up anger toward her overly controlling father by killing him during an argument. Her older siblings had all been poor students with behavior problems, but this girl dutifully obeyed her father's commands to apply herself diligently to her schoolwork and to spend very little time socializing with friends. She was anxious to fulfill her father's dream that a child of his could achieve something great. Whenever she experienced resentment over the fact that she was missing out on a lot of fun that her friends were having, she would redouble her efforts to fulfill her father's expectations. But as much as she tried to please her father, he still found reason to criticize her and during one discussion slapped her face two times. In a fit of rage over what she considered to be his unfair, degrading treatment of her, she got her father's gun and shot him.

Treatment

Individuals who exhibit a sudden breakdown of rigid controls need individual therapy to learn how to deal with their emotions more suitably, as well as family therapy to help them work out conflicts with their parents. In the more severe cases it is appropriate to apply some negative consequences to emphasize the unacceptability of their acting out behavior.

Chapter 7

IMPULSE-RIDDEN PLEASURE SEEKERS

One group of juvenile offenders stands out from the rest in that they usually do not act out their frustrations against others. They are the hedonistic, thrill-seeking, impulse-ridden teenagers whose behavior is beyond parental control and who get heavily involved in drug and sexual activities. In the instances when they commit other crimes such as shoplifting or auto theft, their main motive appears to be pleasure rather than anger. Clinical studies point to low self-esteem, depression, inner emptiness, and a sense of estrangement from others as underlying factors in the overdriven pursuit of fun and excitement.

As one exuberant, outgoing, fun-loving 15-year-old girl with a history of runaways, drug use, and sexual promiscuity explained:

> I try to push away bad things. I try to look at the bright
> side. I just take life day by day. I think both our parents
> are chicken shit. Neither one of them want us. Yeah, they
> want us, but they don't want the responsibility of having
> us. If they could have custody of us, but have someone

else buy our clothes, make sure we get to school, they'd take us in a flash. I know my mom loves us because we're hers, but she hates kids.... She never should have had kids.... The only family relationship I could imagine is me and my brother. He is the only person I feel is family. ... I try to imagine living with my mom, having a mom and daughter relationship. I can't.... I have very few clothes. When my dad sends money for me, my mom takes the check and buys herself clothes. She don't care how I look.... I have a fun life. I enjoy my life, except it's not worth it. I keep getting in trouble. I know I'm messing up. I want to get straight. I don't like how I'm living my life....I don't want trouble and I really try hard, but the trouble jumps in front of me and I take it.

Another thrill-seeking, beyond-control 16-year-old girl could not explain her behavior, but her psychological evaluation revealed that she had a poor self-image and felt somewhat dead inside. In addition, she perceived her home as a cold, forbidding place where she met with nothing but disapproval. While it is debatable which came first, her unruly behavior or her parents' disapproval, her wild behavior seemed to represent an attempt to seek external stimulation and excitement to reduce her inner sense of emptiness, boredom, and depression.

A 14-year-old girl charged with possession of stolen property presented as a lively, fun-loving, pleasure-seeking individual who rarely took things seriously. However, from her remarks it appeared that much of her liveliness was a defense against the unhappiness she was experiencing at home. She complained about her parents' constant criticism of her and indicated she wanted to go anywhere but home. She denied being bothered by the fact that she was adopted, but there were indications that this was also bothering her. Her TAT stories about reunions after long separations seemed to reflect her yearning to be reunited with her natural parents. In addition, her parents' statements that they had done everything for her must have been a reminder that she was not their natural child and they did not have to do anything for her. Psychological testing also revealed her tendency to block out emotional pain by any means possible. Several of her (TAT) stories described unbelievably rapid resolutions to serious problems of failure, rejection, and loss. In addition, her Rorschach presented an interesting contrast. On the one hand, she was bursting with energy; her imagination and emotional reactions were extremely vivid. On the other hand, she expressed a barren, wasted feeling. Apparently, this girl engaged in frenzied acitivity to cover up and avoid facing her underlying unhappiness.

A 15½-year-old boy charged with two counts of theft presented as an extremely pleasure-oriented, fun-loving, excitement-seeking individual. He said he liked girls a lot, but had no desire to develop a close relationship with any particular girl. He would rather have lots and lots of girlfriends, ''at least one for every night of the week.'' He said he loved skateboarding and enjoyed taking dares to do dangerous stunts. ''I love to gamble on everything.'' In the intelligence testing he did best on tasks he could master immediately and poorest on those requiring sustained application of effort. Similarly, he made little effort on the Rorschach to develop percepts, but those he gave showed a high level of thoughtfulness and imagination. A few of his percepts reflected a strong interest in outward appearances, apparently stemming from a need to impress others. There was also evidence in the test data of marked anxiety about bodily harm. In conclusion, it appeared that this boy was driven by some inner emptiness and insecurity to take dangerous risks in order to impress and amaze other people, to prove his worth to himself, and to overcome his anxiety about bodily harm. Though capable of a high level of achievement, he had little interest in anything requiring diligent effort because it did not serve his overriding need to take risks.

In some cases the line between thrill-seeking and self-destructive behavior is very thin. This was particularly true in the case of a 14-year-old girl who had been heavily involved in drug and alcohol abuse as well as prostitution. She had failed to respond to treatment at two different local facilities and was being considered for placement in a state hospital. During her evaluation she admitted to many self-degrading, self-destructive behaviors. For example, she once allowed 13 Marines to have sex with her. At first she was laughing, but then she started crying. Afterwards she felt just horrible. "The number of guys I've had in my life I wouldn't want to count. I am ashamed of myself for what I did. I feel I should hurt myself, like I'm punishing myself." She pointed to some scratches on her arm which she had inflicted when she felt like killing herself. Although she usually hurt herself, rather than others, on several occasions when she was being restrained by the police or juvenile hall staff, she became violent toward them. She indicated that when she was last put in the rubber room in juvenile hall, she sat in a corner sucking her thumb, rocking, and saying over and over, "mommy, mommy." She said she still loved her stepmother even though her stepmother "busted" her teeth and more. "She talked to me. Dad ignored me. He didn't care. . . . I want to see my stepmom again. She's the only person in this world I think loves me." Psychological testing of this girl revealed no gross abnormalities such as primitive mental processes or psychotic ideation. Her reality testing was intact and she displayed many resources indicating a potential for healthy functioning. On the other hand, she displayed a marked difficulty in handling her feelings. When emotionally stressed, she showed a tendency to fly off into uncontrolled behavior without any consideration of consequences. Furthermore, a depressive mood pervaded her TAT stories. It appeared that her depression stemmed in part from a sense of her own defectiveness and in part from a sense of the emptiness of her existence. However, the major portion of her depression seemed to relate to her hopeless yearning to be a little girl again. Her masochistic behavior appeared to be associated with this yearning. As a child she had been severely abused by the only person she felt cared about her (her stepmother). She thus made a connection in her mind between love and attention, and pain and degradation. The only alternative she could imagine was to be totally ignored, something she considered infinitely worse because it made her feel like a nonentity. To avoid that, she set up situations in which she received attention, but at a very heavy price, including physical pain and self-degradation. Afterwards, she would be appalled at how she had allowed herself to be degraded and would proceed to punish herself even further.

Alcohol and Drug Abuse

While alchohol and drug usage is part of the youth culture, most young people exercise sufficient moderation and discretion to avoid arrest. The small percentage of users who are arrested are usually so heavily into alcohol and drugs that they are extremely incautious regarding their health, safety, and the law. They do not use these substances as most people do, merely for recreation and socialization. They seek pleasurable highs or a numbing sensation in order to reduce their awareness of emotional pain. Although they gain the desired effect for a while, their uncontrolled use of alcohol and drugs inevitably produces the opposite effect. Excessive intake of alcohol and drugs makes them less capable of carrying on the business of living, causing them more problems than they had to begin with. Thus, while trying to avoid pain, their behavior paradoxically brings on more pain. Eventually their depression progresses to the point at which their only goal seems to be the hastening of their self-destruction.

In the case of a 17-year-old heavy drug user, his underlying depression appeared to be related to unresolved feelings about his adoption. He said he was informed of his adoption when he was seven and that it had never been a big issue in his life. However, in another context he mentioned that he started being depressed at age seven, a condition that worsened when he was ten, and he started getting into drugs when he was 13. He said he found it depressing hanging around his parents, doing chores and errands. "At the time I think I needed to get away from my everyday life." He became a frequent user of marijuana, speed, and LSD, as well as a heavy drinker. Prior to his detention he was drinking heavily and his only nutrition was the enormous quantity of milk he also drank.

In another case of heavy drug usage a 16-year-old boy initially described his family as great, but as the interview progressed it became more and more apparent that he was deeply troubled by some serious family problems. Ever since the boy was ten, his father openly dated other women while his mother stayed at home by herself steadily drinking. The boy did not know why his parents did not get a divorce, but he did not want that to happen because "both my parents are nice to us kids." He felt sorry for his mother. "It seems like she is getting left out of life," and he did not know how he could remedy the situation.

Both these youths had difficulty facing up to their problems, and when their denial did not work they turned to drugs for comfort.

For some persons who are heavily into the drug culture, the main attraction is not drugs. They use drugs as a way of establishing a bond, a camaraderie with others. They are the loners who desperately want to make contact with others and have never found a way prior to joining the drug scene. There they find a ready acceptance, an easy intimacy because everyone and anyone who uses drugs is welcomed. Of course, this totally unselective intimacy is more apparent than real. But "druggies" fail to realize this because their minds are so beclouded with drugs. Besides, when they are disappointed with one person, they can always find another ersatz intimate to replace the previous one. If any disappointment remains, they can always take more drugs to dull the pain. In this manner they can continue to deceive themselves into thinking that they have found meaningful relationships.

In one case, a 16-year-old boy who was heavily into the drug scene had a real sense of belonging after years of being rather isolated socially. He was jolted to reality when he was busted for a drug sale and discovered that none of the people he considered friends were friends after all. They stopped seeing him and they did not even bother to phone him to find out how he was. As a result, he felt even more socially isolated than ever.

Sexual Acting Out

Juveniles who become involved in uncontrolled sexual behavior, including orgies and prostitution, are very similar to drug abusers. They too go beyond the normal behavior limits to fill an inner emptiness and to lessen their feelings of estrangement from others.

One 15-year-old boy who was arrested for prostitution while a runaway said he did not want to stay at home because he could not get along with his father or little sister.

> I'd rather be on the street and have nobody bossing me around. I'd rather be out there making my own money, be on my own than have my parents with me....I meet people better on the streets, I get along with people better on the streets than in my house. I know people living on the streets making more money than you [the psychologist]. It's not just money, its funner...It's boring down here. I have more friends up there, 20,000 more.

He also expressed great pleasure in knowing how to hustle dinner and a room for the night without even having sex and in helping other kids on the street make money and keep from getting caught. "I'm smart, I can help them" he boasted.

Teenage girls who have tried prostitution speak in similar terms. Whereas most people regard prostitution as a miserable, degrading existence, they see it as a way of increasing their happiness in life and their self-esteem. Some girls have been so emotionally deprived that for them the life of a prostitute is truly self-enhancing. However, others find the experience less rewarding than they expected.

A 13-year-old prostitute who was abandoned by her mother as an infant and then reclaimed when she was 12, found life with her extremely immature mother and her alcoholic, often physically abusive stepfather unbearable. Her eyes glistened with pleasure as she spoke about the excitement of street life, all the people she knew, the pimp's fine clothes and cars, and the fun she had outwitting her "tricks," ripping them off for more than they agreed to pay, sometimes even leaving them before any sex took place. She evidently found a home on the streets more to her liking than any other home she had known.

One 16-year-old girl decided to leave home because she was tired of her dull social life and her mother's constant criticism of her which was at times irrational. She thought running away would be fun. When she couldn't find a job, she decided to prostitute herself rather than return home, sponge off friends, or steal. She wanted, as she proudly put it, "to prove I could make it on my own." However, she discovered prostituting herself made her more depressed than before and she ended up wanting to return home to a straight life.

A 15-year-old girl who was unhappy at home because she could not get along with her stepmother and her father did not give her enough attention, and who was also upset about a broken romance, was convinced by a girlfriend that she would make a great deal of money and lead a glamorous life as a prostitute. Besides, she believed she would be better off than at home because the pimp would take care of her and she wouldn't have to listen to her parents. When she discovered that the pimp took all her money and she got practically nothing in return, she decided it was not worth it.

A 17-year-old girl had started prostituting herself at the age of 14 in order to support herself as a runaway. She rejected the alternative of stealing because she did not want to hurt anybody. However, prostitution was also difficult for her. Raised in a strict religious home, she needed drugs to numb her feelings and overcome her inhibitions. Eventually, what was originally a means to an end became an end in itself. She became addicted to drugs and felt compelled to engage in a higher rate of prostitution in order to support her expensive drug habit.

Treatment

Impulse-ridden pleasure seekers like alcoholics, drug abusers, and prostitutes need help rather than punishment to overcome their self-defeating patterns and discover more satisfying ways of living. Confinement can help to break their undesirable habits, but they will rapidly return to them unless they undergo some inner changes. They need to develop a sense of their intrinsic worth. They need to overcome their inner sense of emptiness and futility.

It is fairly evident why intensive residential treatment or an intensive rehabilitation program like AA is more successful with this population than the traditional outpatient therapies. While therapy can help some impulse-ridden individuals to understand why they do what they do and to bring their behavior under control, many need to learn a whole new life style, a whole new way of relating to others that weekly therapy sessions can hardly begin to provide. Besides, being able to benefit from outpatient therapy requires more of a commitment to change than most impulse-ridden individuals can muster. They are usually enjoying their symptoms too much to want to give them up. Therefore, outpatient treatment should be attempted only if the individual demonstrates a strong determination to change and has a living situation that would support the change.

Chapter 8

LOW FRUSTRATION TOLERANCE

In my experience conducting psychological evaluations of juvenile offenders, low frustration tolerance seems to be the most prevalent cause of juvenile crime. Many juvenile offenders have built up certain sensitivities over time due to frustration in the past. They have never learned to effectively cope with this stress when it appears again. For one thing, they often block off their awareness of their upset feelings. So instead of dealing with their frustrations on a verbal level, in thought or communication, they act upon them with little, if any, conscious control. Furthermore, since they are not fully cognizant of their underlying motivations, they are prone to project blame for their behavior onto others. In this way they deny responsibility for their behavior and at the same time justify it.

Acting-out behavior in cases of low frustration tolerance covers the whole range of delinquent behavior. The form it takes depends upon the individual and his or her situation. For example, stealing is often a reaction to and compensation for feelings of emotional deprivation. Physical aggression is often a reaction to and compensation for feelings of inadequacy.

Running away from family to friends is often a reaction to and compensation for feelings of being misunderstood and not really cared for.

There appear to be two major sources of stress in juvenile crime that are often, though not always, distinct: unsatisfied needs for nurturance and deep-seated feelings of inadequacy and vulnerability.

Unsatisfied Needs for Nurturance

Individuals who feel insufficiently loved are very sensitive to any signs of rejection. Their whole life seems aimed at winning the love and approval they feel they have missed. But unfortunately many of their experiences convince them they are still not receiving the love they so desperately need. One response to this situation is to retreat into a shell to nurse one's wounds. Another response is to actively express one's resentment by repeatedly striking out at others.

A 15½-year-old boy with a history of violent, destructive behavior stated: "I see nothing wrong with fighting. At least you get your anger over with and I like fighting." He also indicated that he had no hesitation about hurting or being hurt, that it is just a risk you run, no greater than the risk you run when you step into a car. He had experienced many traumatic losses in his life. His mother was murdered when he was five. A few years later his baby half-brother drowned, and soon afterward a car accident took the life of his stepmother. Several of his stories on the TAT reflect his feeling that he had been deprived and cheated in life and had been forced to rely solely on himself in order to survive. One story in particular depicts his deep sense of desolation and abandonment: "This guy had so many problems. He thought everyone was against him. He got all depressed. He wondered if anybody cared. He's just wondering if anybody ever cared about him or what happened to him. He's just sad and wondered and felt all hurt."

A 17-year-old girl was arrested for sending threatening and libelous letters to one of her teachers for a period of several months. She indicated that at first she liked the teacher very much and wanted to get close to her. But the teacher, evidently uncomfortable with the girl's interest in her, responded with sarcasm. She accused the girl of glaring at her and told the girl to look in the mirror sometime to see herself. She also told the girl she had a chip on her shoulder. The girl was amazed at the teacher's reactions because she had genuinely liked the teacher and she was doubly hurt when she saw how warm and friendly the teacher was to other students. The whole situation bothered the girl so much she cried more than once about it before she developed the plan of getting back at the teacher. Upon questioning, the girl was reluctant to say anything about her family. At one point, when she was asked if she wished she had a sister, her eyes overflowed with tears, but she would not discuss her feelings. She spontaneously mentioned that she did not really know her brother, he was a stranger to her, and again her eyes filled with tears. When the psychologist mentioned that she appeared to be a very lonely person, she said with surprise that was exactly what her mother told her. She revealed she could not discuss her feelings with her parents because her mother "is always in a daze...she doesn't listen" and her father "is impatient, he twists things."

A 15-year-old girl from a seemingly stable family was a chronic runaway and became, among other things, a heroin user and a participant in Hell's Angels activities. She was hostile and uncooperative during her initial contact with the psychologist. Nevertheless, despite all her resistance to opening up, her eyes frequently filled with tears and at different moments she spilled out some of the things that were bothering her.

> I just never had nobody to talk to...My mom did not seem like she loved me. She kind of ignored me. She paid attention to my sister....I can't talk to my dad either. He's not the type of person who shows his love really....My mom's told me that she hates me. When I started running away and got busted, she'd say, 'Leave, don't come back. I hate you.' She'd say it all the time, screaming it in my face....My father says he doesn't care. He kicked me out....I didn't run away all those times. A couple of times my parents kicked me out [of the

house]. When I didn't come back they'd call the police....Other times my mom would kick me out and when I came back she wouldn't let me in.

A 16-year-old boy who had been detained in juvenile hall on numerous occasions for petty crimes and had been unsuccessfully tried in many out-of-home placements was described by juvenile hall staff as having the worst temper they had ever seen. The slightest frustration would set him off into a rage that could only be controlled by physically restraining him. Whenever he was in the hall he would phone home to ask his mother to visit him. She invariably put him off, by either refusing to come to the phone or by promising to visit, but never actually visiting. He expressed intense anger at her for rejecting him and at his sister whom he felt influenced his mother against him. His stories on the TAT reflect the conflict he experienced with regard to females. He saw females as being warm and affectionate with each other and leaving him out in the cold. Furthermore, although he felt terribly rejected by his mother and acknowledged that it was not a good idea for him to live with her, it was apparent that he still yearned for warmth from her and deep down he still wanted to be back at home with her.

A 13-year-old girl, arrested for petty theft while a runaway, had been a severe problem since the breakup of her parents' marriage when she was nine. It was obvious from her remarks that she felt abandoned by both parents because they each had formed new alliances that superseded their bond with her. First, her mother left her with her father because "she could not afford to take me, but I wanted to go." She didn't get along with her father's new wife who she said would hit her for her misbehavior and remind her that her own mom didn't want her. When she complained about this to her father, the stepmother would deny everything and her father would not believe her. After three years it was arranged for this girl to try living with her mother. The mother was living with a lover and when the lover's child complained about something this girl did, this girl felt her mother automatically sided with the other child. Although this girl might have been exaggerating the

unfair treatment she received, both parents' extremely negative statements about her lent credence to her belief that she
had been emotionally abandoned in favor of her parents' new
partners.

A 15-year-old girl who had been in a variety of out-of-
home placements since the age of nine because of her beyond-
control and assaultive behavior expressed intensely negative
feelings about the way her life had been going thus far. She bitterly complained that her mother put her live-in boyfriend
ahead of her own children. Shortly after he moved in, this girl
ran away and her younger brother and sister went to live with
their father because they did not like the mother's boyfriend
disciplining them. This girl felt her mother did not care that
three of her four children left and was not glad when they
returned. In her opinion, her mother continued to stand by the
boyfriend in everything and never took her children's side.
Nevertheless, this girl was insistent that she would rather
return home than go to a foster home or a 24-hour school. She
said foster homes are supposed to treat you like a member of
the family, but in her experience they do not. She did not want
to go to a 24-hour school because she was sick of institutional
living. From all the things she said and from the way she said
them, it was clear that this girl was an intensely emotional individual who had suffered many hurts in the past. As a result, she
carried a lot of anger inside her and tended to have quick,
strong reactions to situations. However, she was not rigid or
inflexible in her viewpoint. If dealt with in a nonassertive manner, she was open to other points of view. In line with this
observation, she stated that she responded much better to
requests than to demands. Psychological testing revealed an
intense yearning for affection and closeness and bitter frustration that she was not getting these needs fulfilled. Her drawing
of a female figure was that of an angry, withholding older
woman whose bosom seemed more like a weapon than a source
of comfort. Moreover, her drawing of a house resembled a
large fortress that was barricaded against easy entrance, the
exact opposite of a welcoming home. These drawings power-
fully demonstrated the feelings she had expressed about her
own mother and her own home.

Feelings of Inadequacy and Vulnerability

Individuals with deep-seated feelings of inadequacy and vulnerability are supersensitive to anything that threatens their self-confidence and they overreact to anything they interpret as a put down. Their whole life seems aimed at compensating for their felt inadequacies and proving they are persons of importance, persons of strength, persons to be reckoned with. When they are not given the respect they believe they deserve, they angrily strike out at others. In addition, they perceive any deferral to authority figures as extremely demeaning. While a certain amount of rebelliousness is a normal part of adolescence, these adolescents regard anything less than complete autonomy as total submision.

One 13-year-old boy who was a chronic truant from school and had also been involved in some thefts, was being considered for an out-of-home placement. Although his home environment had been known for years to Welfare and Dependency as substandard, materially and psychologically, no previous action had been taken to remove the children because it was felt there was not a sufficient case to warrant such action. In the interview this boy explained his truancy in terms of his being bored and nervous at school because he did not understand the work. He felt this was due to his family's frequent moves and his never having had a chance to learn what he was supposed to learn. He said he wanted to complete his high school education, but his way, not the way they do it in school. When asked what was his way, he admitted he did not know. Sometime later in the interview, however, he said he would like to work at his own pace with a home teacher to bring his level up so he could eventually return to a regular school. He added that he could work much better with music playing because, with so many things going on in his head, he needed music to calm down. He also expressed a strong desire to find regular employment. He believed he was qualified as a mechanic and he greatly resented the fact that no one would hire him because of his age. In the course of discussing a possible out-of-home placement, he expressed strong feelings against the govern-

ment for trying to run his life and mess up his mind. Psychological testing revealed that the boy had a very poor self-image,
was extremely fearful of close emotional involvements, and was
very resistant to authority figures. Evidently, this boy's intense
need to maintain control of his life was due to his underlying
feelings of weakness and inadequacy.

In a similar case, a 16-year-old girl who was arrested for
assaulting a school security guard after he ordered her off
school grounds presented herself as extremely independent and
resistant to any external controls. Nevertheless, her choice of
the animal she would most like to be pointed to opposite feelings: "A dog because they have people to take care of them.
They never have to worry about anything.... It doesn't
matter what animal you'd be changed into. It matters who is
taking care of you." Evidently, this girl's intense striving for
autonomy and low tolerance of control by others masked deep-
rooted dependency needs which she consciously rejected
because they signified weakness to her.

A 16-year-old boy who was arrested for receiving stolen
property following an earlier arrest for burglary, was very
upset about being detained in juvenile hall because of the loss
of income from his job and the possibility of losing his job alto-
gether. Just how significant this was to him became clearer and
clearer as the interview progressed. Although his parents were
financially comfortable and willing to give him spending
money, the most important thing in life to him was to earn his
own money. When he was deprived of the chance to do so he
was absolutely miserable. He had recently been laid off from
one job and he could not stand having no money coming in, so
he decided to engage in burglaries until he could obtain
another job. When he worked he willingly sacrificed his education, recreation, and social relations in order to work as many
hours as possible. At school he took the bare minimum of
required courses even though he was planning on going to col-
lege and recently he was thinking of dropping out of school so
he could work at his job full-time and earn a dollar more per
hour. He did not go anywhere with other boys because he
thought it was a waste of time. "The only person I hang

around with is my girlfriend.'' Upon questioning, he could not describe what he liked about her, but he proudly mentioned that her parents like him a lot and he spends a lot of money on her, taking her out and buying her clothing. From the way he spoke it appeared that he had been going with this girl for a long time. Therefore, it was rather surprising to learn that he had only known her for a month. Evidently, the boy lacked confidence in his ability to establish peer relationships. Consequently, he latched onto this girl and invested their relationship with a great deal of meaning mainly because the girl and her parents accepted him. Besides, with money to spend on her, he felt confident he could maintain her interest in him. Thus, earning money served the double purpose of covering up his inadequacies in other areas and providing him with the emotional security of a relationship he felt powerless to maintain otherwise.

A 14½-year-old boy was arrested for shooting a BB gun at cars, then beating up a man. He was willing to discuss the offense and he was willing to take the tests, but he made it clear he would not discuss his feelings or anything to do with his family. He asserted that his family had nothing to do with his offense; he was the only one responsible for his actions. He related that a friend asked him to join him in shooting BBs in a field beside his house. He knew it was against the law to shoot where people could be hit, but he thought the field was a safe place to shoot, so he agreed. A passing truck stopped and the driver said that one of the BBs made a dent in his truck. The man grabbed the gun and held it on the boys while his wife went to phone the police. While waiting for the police to arrive, the man berated the boys with such comments as: ''You scum, you punks.'' After listening to this a while, this boy felt he could not take it any longer. He was afraid to leave because he believed the man would shoot him, so he did the only thing he could think of. He punched the man whereupon the man threw him down and started wrestling with him. In the psychological testing this boy was very guarded, giving mostly bland, conventional responses. Nevertheless, a few of his responses were quite revealing. They showed him to be extremely preoccupied with aggression, both as the aggressor and as the object of aggression. It appeared that life was a struggle for him and he was tired of fighting for his existence. He seemed to want to be so strong and so secure that he would not have to always be on guard just to survive. A few of his test responses suggested that he had severe difficulties relating to his father. He seemed to perceive his father as a powerful, dangerous figure who threatened his safety. Apparently, the recent incident in which this boy punched a man for cursing him was not an isolated incident as this boy wanted to believe. Rather, it seemed to be an expression of the rage he had long felt regarding the verbal and physical abuse he had apparently suffered from his father. Supersensitive to any type of insult or injury, he had evidently taken the position that he would never again stand for any kind of abuse from anyone.

A 15-year-old girl was arrested for stabbing a girl three times. The victim had reportedly been harassing her. Upon questioning about the incident, the girl stated: "I did it to save myself. There were two of them, just me by myself. Both of them had weapons. . . . I was afraid when they came up to me. That's probably why I did it. . . . I seen her weapon. She pulled it out. [Do you feel guilty for hurting her?] I don't feel guilty at all. I felt I had to do it. [Why were you carrying a knife?] Something told me to take it. I never bring a knife with me." Intelligence testing of this girl showed her to be of Dull Normal intelligence with extremely poor understanding of social interactions. Projective testing showed her to be emotionally constricted, but otherwise quite normal. There was no evidence of a thought disorder, intense rage, or poor impulse control. However, she did reveal a strong sense of vulnerability to attack and a strong wish to be able to defend herself. As the animal she would most like to be, she chose a bear "because they're pretty and because they catch their food easy and they know how to protect themselves." As the animal she would least like to be she chose "a cat because people are always stepping on them and kicking them around." Evidently, this girl had truly felt she was in great danger when the two girls confronted her and she believed the stabbing was a necessary defense. Her poor understanding of social interactions sug gested that her assessment of the situation might have been incorrect.

A 15½-year-old girl was a runaway while on probation for a minor offense. Her parents were in the midst of a stormy divorce and the girl exhibited hostile, beyond control behavior in both parents' homes. A psychological evaluation was requested to determine what type of out-of-home placement would be most suitable. In the interview the girl expressed intense anger and contempt toward her parents. She said she did not mind being in juvenile hall and in fact preferred it to being with her parents. The test data, however, indicated feel ings of weakness and vulnerability, rather than hostility. There were several indications that she was feeling overwhelmed and unable to cope with problems in her environment. Further more, her feelings of inadequacy were beginning to generalize making her feel like a complete failure. Evidently, this girl characteristically expressed hostility as a defense against feeling vulnerable. However, this defense did not work well. It only provoked the anger of others which led to her feeling even more threatened, more of a victim than before.

The following is an example of someone who exhibited frustration over feeling both rejected and inadequate.

A 15½-year-old boy was arrested for trying to strangle a female student near school. While detained in juvenile hall his behavior went out of control and he was placed in seclusion. He was still very agitated when the psychologist came to speak to him and he expressed intense feelings of self-loathing. "I am insane. . . . I am a failure. . . . I am dangerous. . . . I want to kill myself. . . . I should be locked up in an insane asylum and shot by a firing squad." When asked why he thought he was a failure, he said he was a failure with girls. Then he expressed defeatist attitudes toward everything in his life. From the time he started school he felt he could not do the work so he did not try (even though IQ tests showed him to have above average potential). In social settings he always assumed nobody would like him (even though he showed himself to be quite witty and likable in subsequent interviews). He said he would like to have a lot of money, but he was too lazy to work for it. He claimed he had no goals or ambitions in life other than to have a girl-friend. But he knew girls did not like him because he was too rough and he got into too many fights. Questioning about his attempted strangling of the girl revealed that he wanted her to be his girlfriend. The day of the strangling, he had joined her and a friend of her's at lunch. At one point he put his hand on her shoulders in a friendly gesture, but she pushed his hands off and picked up her purse to leave. He grabbed her purse and told her to sit down, whereupon she flung her hand at his stomach. This hurt him, both physically and emotionally, and in anger he grabbed her around the neck.

Treatment

The appropriate treatment of individuals who act out as a result of their low frustration tolerance naturally depends upon the severity and frequency of their acting-out behavior. In some cases a court appearance and probation are sufficient measures to ward off a recurrence of the acting-out behavior. In other, more serious cases, some sort of confinement is advisable to emphasize the fact that that behavior is simply not acceptable. In all cases, however, counseling or therapy is also strongly advised to help the individual develop more mature mechanisms to cope with frustration.

Chapter 9

IMMATURE PERSONALITIES

The major characteristic of some juvenile offenders is their extreme social immaturity. Their acting-out behavior is not motivated by delinquent attitudes or marked psychological disturbance. Nor do they show signs of primitive mental processes. What gets them in trouble is their dependency, their poor social skills, and their poor judgment. Frequently bored and eager for something to do, often lonely and craving human companionship, they are easily led by anyone who takes the time to befriend them. Though immature youngsters lack the social skills needed to develop ordinary age-appropriate friendships, criminally oriented individuals often find them ideal companions for their purposes. Immature youngsters, happy to be accepted at last and eager to maintain their new "friendships," loyally follow wherever their delinquent mentors lead, never stopping to consider the right or wrong of their actions or possible negative consequences to themselves.

For example, a 16-year-old boy with no prior criminal record and two companions with prior records stole an $8,000 truck. After the owner recovered the truck, this boy set it on fire to destroy any evidence that could link him to the theft. He was referred for a psychological evaluation to assess his mental status and possible need for counseling. Upon meeting this boy it was easy to see why the probation officer referred him for an evaluation. He had an exceedingly passive, bland look about him and he seemed much younger than his age. Upon questioning, he could not explain why he stole the truck in the first place. "I don't know. Just something to do." Psychological testing showed him to be of normal intelligence with notable inner resources. He had a vivid imagination in the context of good reality testing. On the other hand, the data indicated that he tended to behave impulsively when emotionally aroused. In addition, he viewed life as a difficult struggle and himself as too young and too incomplete to cope. After receiving some feedback on the test findings, this boy opened up and shared some of his concerns. Socially, he had had several experiences of friends abandoning him, and he was too shy to even begin a relationship with a girl. School was also a frustration to him. He knew he could do the work if he applied himself, but it seemed like so much of a hassle that he frequently would not even try. At home, he was bothered by his mother's frequent yelling at him and was worried by his father's refusal to take care of a serious health condition. All in all, this boy was not getting much pleasure in life. He sought the company of boys wilder than himself, in hopes that they would create some fun for him. In the recent incident he discovered to his dismay that the consequences of wild behavior were not at all fun.

Another 16-year-old boy with a long record of minor offenses expressed a strong belief that he would not have gotten into all this trouble if he had only had a father, or at least an older brother. He believed his mother could not give him the companionship he needed to stay out of trouble. He said he joined friends in delinquent acts because he wanted their company and did not want to be "left out and alone." He mentioned that he recently learned his father's name from his birth certificate, but his mother refused to give him any more information. This bothered him greatly, especially since his 13-year-old brother had started seeing his father the year before. To make matters worse, the brother flaunted his good fortune and teased this boy for not having a father. At this point in the interview this 16-year-old boy started crying. At first he ashamedly tried to hide his tears, but before long he was openly sobbing and wanting to end the interview. Previous psychological testing showed him to have above average intellectual potential and well-developed perceptions and imagination, but difficulty in dealing with feelings. He appeared insecure, feeling alone and helpless, and he did not view his home as a place of sustenance and strength. It seemed likely that his delinquent acts were intended to impress people and to make them like him.

A 14½-year-old girl who had been staying out nights and truanting school continually lied her way into and out of situations in an effort to appear older and to get her way. She was referred for an evaluation to determine her level of intellectual functioning and the adequacy of her reality resting. Psychological testing revealed immaturity, but no serious defect or pathology. She tested in the low-average range of intelligence, but her thinking was shallow and her understanding of different situations superficial. Like a young child, she tended to dream up stereotypic, wishful solutions to problems, instead of dealing with them in practical, realistic terms. However, she did not give evidence of an actual psychosis. Her perceptions were not distorted and her associations were not bizarre. Her test responses showed her to be an insecure individual who perceived her home environment as very unnurturing and unsupportive. As a result, she had a strong need to set up external support systems through which she could have her needs met. Apparently, this was the impetus of her frequent lying.

A 17½-year-old boy had been arrested four times in the space of three months for various thefts. Each time he cried profusely and begged for another chance. He blamed his actions on his excessive drinking and he blamed his excessive drinking on the fact that everyone in his neighborhood drank a lot. However, upon further questioning he admitted that not everyone in his neighborhood drank as much as he did, and those who did avoided the kind of trouble he got into. Further discussion revealed that this boy did not feel he fit in with the other boys in his inner city neighborhood. They were much more sophisticated and tougher than those with whom he grew up in a farm community and he engaged in drinking and stealing in an effort to gain acceptance in his new peer group. The drinking built up his confidence and the stealing was to impress others. However, he felt regret after each time he stole something, and was so worried about being caught that his friends would tell him he was "paranoid." This boy expressed a strong wish for external controls on his behavior. He thought being on probation would help, but he was disappointed to find that his probation officer spent very little time with him and did not give him the counseling he expected. This boy also expressed a wish to be closer to his father. "We don't really talk that much. Most of the time we only talk if I get in trouble." He believed he never would have gotten into trouble if his family had not moved from a small town in another state and he wished they had not. Moreover, he felt everyone in his family regretted the move because it did not bring the financial gains they expected and all the children in the family had difficulty adjusting to city life. Psychological testing confirmed the clinical impression of this boy as a somewhat pathetic, depressed individual. He felt weak and lacked confidence in his abilities, even though his psychological resources were at least average. The test data also supported his belief that he would not have done the things he did that got him in trouble if he had not been drunk. Generally conventional in his outlook on life, his basic nature was introverted, passive, and overcontrolled rather than impulsive or action oriented. For example, when a character in one of his TAT stories felt annoyed with something, he tended to be passively resistant, instead of openly rebellious. There was also evidence that he yearned to be protected and taken care of like a young child and that he did not feel at all ready for the responsibilities of adult life.

A 17-year-old girl charged with abandoning her day-old baby under a bush explained that she left the baby for just a short time while she went shopping for diapers. She had kept the pregnancy a secret and had not yet had the courage to tell anyone about the birth. Although her action of leaving a day-old baby under a bush suggested severe mental and/or emotional problems, the psychological evaluation revealed some immaturity, but nothing seriously amiss. Her intelligence was not subnormal, her personality development was not primitive, and she was not severely disturbed. Moreover, her act of endangering her baby was completely out of character for her inasmuch as she was a kindhearted individual who had taken good care of many other babies in the past. Evidently, her judgment had been clouded in this situation by her desire to keep her illegitimate pregnancy a secret as long as possible. Her tendency to retreat from emotionally trying situations instead of dealing with them or seeking help from others was also noted in the test data.

Treatment

To stop their delinquent activities, immature juvenile offenders need to learn to think about the consequences of their actions, both to themselves and to others. In most cases it is suitable to attempt counseling before taking stronger measures. Immature juvenile offenders also need to improve their social skills and develop satisfying recreational activities so they will not be so susceptible to delinquent leadership. "Big Brother" or "Big Sister" volunteers who can spend time with the immature offenders and organized group activities can be very helpful in this regard. If counseling and structured leisure time activities are not sufficient intervention to stop the delinquent activities, a total change of environment is necessary. In that case the immature offenders should be placed in a foster home or 24-hour school where they can receive both the supervision they need to stay out of trouble and the nurturing they need to mature.

Chapter 10

INADEQUATE PERSONALITIES

The psychological development of some juvenile offenders is severely stunted by marked inborn intellectual limitations and/or extreme emotional deprivation. Lacking the inner resources and social tools to cope with many of life's demands, they experience numerous frustrations in their daily lives. At best their adjustment in society is marginal; at worst they are very disruptive, repeatedly acting out their frustrated needs in various socially unacceptable ways.

Juvenile offenders with inadequate personalities resemble the juvenile offenders with low frustration tolerance in that they also exhibit a low tolerance for stress. The main difference between the two is that the frustrations in the former group arise from actual inadequacies whereas those in the latter group arise from felt inadequacies that are not real, i.e., neurotic perceptions about themselves.

Inadequate personalities resemble immature personalities in that they too are immature. The difference between them lies in the depth of their immaturity. The psychological development of the inadequate personalities is so stunted that their overall functioning is primitive. Immature personalities, on the other hand, are basically intact psychologically, though socially immature.

Cases of Inborn Mental Deficiency

A 17-year-old boy charged with the kidnapping and sexual molestation of a four-year-old boy was referred for psychological evaluation because of suspected mental retardation. He was a gentle-looking boy who seemed much younger than his age. He related to the psychologist like a docile child and readily accepted the demands of the testing situation. Although he applied himself diligently to every task, he expressed no concern about how well he was doing and seemed blithely unaware of his failures. Testing revealed that his overall intellectual functioning was on the Mentally Deficient level and his potential was probably not much higher than the Borderline level. The projective tests indicated that his emotional development had been arrested at a very young level and his interests were extremely childish. Even his interest in sex, with which he showed a marked preoccupation, was basically childish. While his reality testing was essentially good, it tended to break down under the impact of strong emotional stimuli. He displayed no capacity to utilize emotional stimuli in adaptive ways or even to express his own feelings. He tried to ignore emotions and when he could not his perceptions became distorted. He apparently had great difficulty in social interactions and had little ability to form close relationships. He gave no indication of aggressive impulses. Basically he appeared to be a very inadequate, passive individual.

A 13½-year-old unwed mother who assaulted a girl with a knife in front of a teacher and other students was referred for a psychological evaluation because she had difficulty understanding and following the rules in a rehabilitation center. She was evaluated over three sessions and each time she showed an entirely different side of her personality. The first time she passively complied with the demands of the testing situation, showing no affect. At the second session she was very grouchy and complained about having to take tests. At the third session she was in a very cheerful, agreeable mood and was quite charming. She appeared to be a simple-minded person who pretty much took life as it came and did not think too deeply or too long on any one subject, even though she was capable of strong feelings at the time something was happening. When questioned as to her feelings about having a baby at her young age, she said: "I felt terrible at the time," but then added, "It was just a mistake. It had to happen. . . . It's life." She humorously related that her mother told her that she "should have kept her dress down and her pants up." Then she described with obvious pleasure how her mother treated her "like a baby" as soon as she knew about the pregnancy. Testing showed this girl to be functioning in the Mentally Deficient range of intelligence. Her projective test responses reflected severe emotional impoverishment as well as intellectual deficiency. She demonstrated an extreme lack of perceptual differentiation, imagination, and ability to organize details into meaningful patterns. However, one response indicated sensitivity to emotional stimuli and an ability to express emotions in socially adaptive ways. There was no indication in the test data of emotional explosiveness or the kind of assaultive behavior with which she was charged. The responses she did give suggested frustration over unfulfilled needs for nurturance. Her childish house and tree drawings, complete with a smiling sun and pretty flowers, seemed to reflect her yearning for the childhood delights of which she apparently did not get enough.

A 17½-year-old girl, referred for an evaluation after assaulting her foster mother during an argument, seemed the antithesis of hostility with her soulful eyes and sweet smile. The results of the psychological evaluation indicated that her physical aggression was not due to strong hostile impulses, but rather to the frustration of not being able to adequately express herself in words. Intellectually she was functioning on the Borderline Retarded level. Socially she had the capacity for warm relationships, but her practical judgment and understanding of cause and effect sequences was far below her age level. Emotionally she did not display any gross disturbances, but in many ways she was like a young child. For example, she seriously planned on becoming a professional ice skater even though she had gone ice skating only once in her life. She refused to consider more practical ways of making a living. Though she was nearly 18 it was obvious that she was no more ready to go out on her own than a child of ten.

Cases of Below Average Intelligence Compounded by Environmental Deprivation

A 14-year-old runaway girl was arrested for being a lookout while five male friends beat up and robbed a man of $2.00. At the time of her evaluation she was a physical mess, with a black eye and cigarette burns on her arms. Upon questioning, she said she ran away from home because she had no freedom there and, until she had a fight with a guy and woke up the next morning with a black eye, she had liked her life away from home, taking drugs and partying. She couldn't remember how she got the cigarette burns, but she thought a "chick" who was mad at her gave them to her while she was "out" on drugs. Halfway through the testing she spontaneously mentioned: "I'm married to a husband and he doesn't know I am in here." Upon questioning she stated:

> We married the day we ran into each other. We knew each other in grade school. He is 20. We were in the fourth grade because he flunked. He doesn't know I'm 14.... We didn't get a license. It's a common marriage.... When we had money we would stay in a motel. Other times he would stay with friends and I would stay at a hospitality center for people with no money.

Psychological testing showed her to be of Dull Normal intelligence with few inner resources. Her reactions tended to be global and impulsive. She demonstrated little ability to differentiate fine details or to organize the details of her experience. Though her imagination was generally very limited and her emotional reactions very constricted, at times her imagination would run wild and her emotional reactions were uncontrolled. She seemed to yearn to be loved and cared for, but instead felt like a creature who was reviled, attacked, and destroyed by others.

A 16-year-old girl with an assault charge had been an extreme behavior problem in a rehabilitation program and was referred for psychological evaluation for the purpose of placement planning. In the program she had exhibited markedly contrasting behavior. With the psychologist she had seemed very sweet and simple. She smiled and laughed frequently, was eager for sessions, but had very little of substance to say. With the staff she had been extremely uncooperative in a passive resistant manner. When she was put in her room as a punishment, she would say she didn't care, she liked it there. With her peers she was overtly aggressive. Whenever someone was being teased or laughed at, she jumped in and became one of the chief tormentors. She also picked many fights on her own. Realizing that she was prone to violence and unconcerned with consequences, the other girls tried to avoid confrontations with her. Nevertheless, several of them were caught fighting with her, an action which greatly upset them, for each one received an added week in the program as punishment. The girl under discussion, meanwhile, unconcernedly received numerous added weeks. Psychological testing indicated that this girl's intellectual functioning was at the Borderline Retarded level, and her potential was not much higher. Her reality testing was intact, but her psychological development was arrested at an extremely immature level. She was interested in interpersonal relationships, but her poorly differentiated perceptions and her shallow emotions kept her from having anything but the most superficial contact. She was very much like the human figures she drew with elaborate clothing and blank looking faces. While she may have possessed some surface qualities to fit in with her peers, she was fairly empty inside and had little of substance to offer any relationship. In addition, she was filled with many childish fears of unknown terrors that might be lurking in the world outside.

Cases of Severely Stunted Personality Development in Individuals With Normal Intellectual Potential

A 12½-year-old boy, who was a frequent runaway and petty thief while on the run, appeared very disheveled at the time of his evaluation. His hair was going in all directions and a closer look revealed that it was also irregular in length. He explained that he keeps running away because his mother "pulls my hair and stuff" whenever she gets drunk, which happens "almost every day." Psychological testing indicated that his intellectual functioning was average, but his personality development was severely stunted (at the level of a four- or five-year-old child). Although he was very responsive to the emotional impact of the different test stimuli, he could do little with his emotional reactions. He mostly described what he saw and used little imagination or intellect to organize the details into meaningful patterns. It appeared from several of his responses that he had a deep sense that he was not a whole person, that he was missing or lacking something.

A 16-year-old boy was referred for psychological evaluation for possible out-of-home placement because of his repeated burglaries of neighbors' homes, cars, and mailboxes. This boy appeared more like a 13-year-old than a 16-year-old. He had an earnest, worried look upon his face, a far cry from the look of a tough delinquent or even a "cool" teenager. Upon questioning, he said he had committed about ten burglaries over three years and the most he ever took was $4.00. He used the money to buy candy and cigarettes. His eyes filled with tears when he described the great anxiety he experienced on entering the homes he burglarized and he expressed relief that the probation department was going to do something to stop him. From his description of his home situation it was apparent that he was lost in the shuffle of a large, chaotic family. Psychological testing revealed an inadequately developed personality. Although there were indications that his intellectual potential was in the Normal range, his verbal functioning was Borderline Retarded. His drawings were so rudimentary they resembled those of a first grader. He responded to the TAT like a young child, describing what he saw in the pictures, but never developing any stories as requested. On the Rorschach he gave good responses to separate details, demonstrating good reality testing, but he displayed no ability to organize disparate details into meaningful perceptions. He also gave no evidence of the capacity to introspect and delay impulses.

A 17-year-old girl with a long history of runaways and a recent assault had a bland, pleasant manner and did not appear at all belligerent. Psychological testing showed her to have normal intellectual potential, but an inadequately developed personality, with limited inner resources to cope with the demands of her environment. In all likelihood, her running away behavior was related to her limited imagination and constricted emotional expression. Whenever she had difficulty getting along with others, she would not try to figure out what she could do to get along better or engage in intense emotional interactions to get her feelings across. She would simply leave the situation.

A 14½-year-old boy who received minimal care and supervision from his alcoholic mother was referred for a psychological evaluation after he started stealing. This boy looked more like 10 or 11 than his actual age. From his reactions during the discussion of a possible foster home placement, it was apparent that his emotional maturity was at an even younger level than his physical appearance. He started sucking his thumb and crying like a small child: "I want to stay with my mama." He said he did not care if his mother was too drunk to take care of him or to keep the house clean. Sometime later, however, he admitted that he feels "kinda miserable" when his mother gets drunk. Testing showed that his intellectual functioning was in the Borderline Retarded range though there were indications in this evaluation and in a previous one of average potential. Evidently, negative environmental factors seriously hindered his intellectual development. His house-tree-person drawings were so rudimentary, they looked more like those of a six- or seven-year-old than like those of a 14½-year-old. His perceptions on the Rorschach were similarly undeveloped. His performance on the more structured TAT was more adequate in that he was able to appropriately interpret major themes of the pictures. However, his elaborations of these themes point to feelings of severe deprivation: "They're trying to grow some food so they don't starve no more. . . . He's crying because he can't get no job. . . . She thinks things will get worse instead of better." In all likelihood, this boy's stealing was related to the severe deprivation he experienced.

A 14-year-old boy charged with assaulting another boy during an argument over his bicycle had been previously charged with assaulting a school principal during a disagreement over his skateboard. Psychological testing showed him to have limited inner resources to cope with conflict. His verbal functioning was on the retarded level, though there was evidence that his intellectual potential was close to average. In addition, he displayed little imagination and he seemed to have no constructive outlet for his feelings. In view of all these limitations it was not surprising that this boy characteristically became violent when frustrated. Questioning revealed that he saw nothing really wrong with his behavior. Although he realized it did not get him what he wanted and instead got him in trouble, he seemed to feel it was the only thing he could have done in the situation.

A 15-year-old boy charged with entering a neighbor's home and taking the woman's underwear and "adult" magazines appeared at first glance to be a tall, well-built, handsome youth. However, after a few moments of observing his facial expression and the way he carried his body, he looked more like a big, overgrown baby. This latter impression was supported by his extremely immature way of relating. Throughout the evaluation he chattered away, asking lots of questions like a young child. Whenever any fairly obvious thing was pointed out to him, he would strongly agree and act as if a great discovery had been made. His obvious anxiety about taking the tests was commented upon and he acknowledged this to be true, stating that he felt he had to do well on the tests or else he would be put in juvenile hall. When he was told that this was not likely unless he was arrested for another crime, he showed tremendous relief and earnestly stated, "I'll never do it again." This boy indicated he had been picked on by other kids at school, but not so much lately, and he had friends in his neighborhood. When questioned about his relationships with girls, he said, "I don't feel comfortable around girls and they don't feel comfortable around me." Then he quickly denied what he considered to be any unseemly interest in them by stating: "I don't want to do anything with them. Of course if I'm married or a girlfriend threatens to break up or she asks..." Further discussion revealed this boy's extreme ignorance about the development of heterosexual relationships. Psychological testing indicated significant psychological impairment of his innate average intellectual potential. In particular, he seemed to have great difficulty interpreting cause and effect sequences in social interactions. On the Rorschach he had great difficulty organizing his perceptions into meaningful responses. He appeared to be almost completely unable to cope with new, unstructured situations where he had no experience to draw upon and where there were no clear behavioral guidelines. When some of the common higher-level percepts were suggested to him, he still could not see them. Thus he demonstrated great difficulty dealing with complex situations, even when appropriate responses were suggested to him. These findings paralleled his social retardation with regard to heterosexual relationships: So far he had not been able to figure out for himself how they work—or even to learn from other people's examples. This boy was much better able to handle the other, more structured projective tests. In fact, aside from expressing feelings of weakness, vulnerability, and a perception of himself as a very little helpless child, his responses on these tests were quite ordinary.

Treatment

Inadequate personalities need greatly enriched environments to help them overcome the damaging effects of their inborn limitations and/or early emotional deprivation. If this can be accomplished while living at home through special programs in the community, that is fine. However, in most cases, due either to a lack of suitable community resources or to overwhelming problems in the home environment, a residential treatment placement is necessary. If no attempt is made to help these individuals to improve their level of functioning when they are young, they will continue to be serious problems in society and may even require institutional care as adults.

Chapter 11

SCHIZOID PERSONALITIES

Some juvenile crimes are so bizarre, the mental state of the offender is immediately called into question. Psychological evaluations commonly show these individuals to be schizoid (either borderline psychotic or prepsychotic). Emotionally withdrawn and socially isolated, they retreat into an inner world of fantasy to obtain the emotional gratification they do not receive in real life. For example, feeling like a miserable failure in every endeavor, the schizoid individual may fantasize that he is a great person, admired by all.

A bizarre crime occurs when the ordinarily passive, schizoid individual develops an uncontrollable urge to act out one of his fantasies in real life. Unlike an actual schizophrenic who cannot distinguish between fantasy and reality, the schizoid individual knows the difference and realizes it is not socially acceptable to act out his fantasies. However, his affect is so blunted and his judgment so impaired, he does not fully grasp the seriousness of his actions.

For example, a 17-year-old boy was referred for a psychological evaluation after being charged with eight counts of arson while a member of his local volunteer fire department.

This boy gave the immediate impression of being out of step with his peers. There was a look and air of innocence about him similar to that of a young child. On the other hand, his serious manner of speaking and way of phrasing things made him seem like a member of the older generation. Upon questioning, he admitted he had difficulty making friends and was socially isolated. He joined the volunteer fire department for the activity and social contact it could provide. However, since the fire department was not active enough to meet his needs, he decided to remedy the situation by setting some fires of his own. He was careful to set fires only in deserted areas where he thought no one could be hurt. Afterwards, he would run to be the first volunteer at the first station. Unlike most arsonists who are excited by the fire itself, this boy was excited at the prospect of putting it out. Psychological testing revealed that he was of Normal intelligence, but that his thinking was peculiar and confused and his perceptions distorted, though not to the extent of full-blown psychosis. He seemed to completely lack internal controls. Apparently, the only controls on his behavior were external ones. Furthermore, though he was sensitive to emotional stimuli, he gave no evidence of socially adaptive emotional responses.

A 17-year-old Navy recruit was arrested in a park for assault after he pushed a woman down and jumped on top of her, simulating sexual intercourse. He had all of his clothes on and did not attempt to take off the victim's clothes. Later he reported having no memory of this incident. It was hard for him to believe he had acted in this manner because it was so out of character for him. Extremely shy, he normally would not even have the courage to speak to a female with whom he was not acquainted, even though he was very interested in finding a girlfriend. All he remembered of that day was that at about 11:30 a.m. he was lying on the grass, thinking about home, and the next thing he knew he awoke in a police car at about 5:00 p.m. wondering and then asking what he was doing there. Upon questioning he admitted that he frequently daydreamed and withdrew into himself, even when he was in a crowd. Furthermore, he was known to be a lone wolf who kept his feelings to himself. Psychological testing showed him to be of superior intelligence though severely emotionally disturbed. Intense anxiety pervaded his test responses. It appeared that he was anxious about nearly every aspect of his existence. In particular, he felt very threatened by interpersonal relationships. He yearned for acceptance, but he felt rejected. Although he saw people as cruel and he believed they should be nice, he blamed their rejection of him on his own weaknesses. Feeling unable to form the close relationships he desired, he tended to emotionally isolate himself from others as protection against further hurt. In the process he made the possibility of a close relationship even more remote. He sought comfort in fantasy, but his fantasy life was not really satisfying. Moreover, his withdrawal into fantasy impaired his reality testing. Apparently this is what happened in the incident in the park. While in a partial dream state he bizarrely acted out his fantasy of getting close to a female which his shyness had prevented him from achieving in reality.

A 16-year-old girl charged with burning down her parents' apartment appeared deeply depressed at the time of her evaluation. However, she did not display any acute signs of depression such as tears or intense remorse. Her depression, as evidenced by the lifeless, washed-out look on her face and her exceedingly flat affect, appeared to be of longstanding duration. Upon questioning, however, she insisted that she was now happy.

> I'm happier here [in juvenile hall] than on the outs. Sometimes I'd get so depressed, I'd sleep for three days. Everyone doesn't like to be locked up, but I won't want to get out. I do crazy things. I'm afraid. I want some help.... When I'm drunk I do things.... When I do something, it just happens. I didn't plan to burn my house. I just did it.... I don't remember burning my house, but I know I did it.... When I drink I feel I can do anything I want to. I feel strong enough.

When asked if she would have done those things if she had not been drinking, she said she probably wouldn't have, then added: "But, I think about doing it. It's all my own ideas. I just do it when I drink." She then went on to describe her fascination with destruction and how she became good friends with another girl in juvenile hall charged with the murder and injury of several persons during a sniping incident.

> One day I said to her, it's just like I've known her a long time, like always. It's weird. And she likes Charlie too.... I was reading a book about the Family, Charles Manson. It fascinates me. I like reading it. Sometimes I wish I was there.... Do you want to know what I did to a cat? I stabbed a cat to death because I wanted to murder something. At first I didn't have any feelings. Now it doesn't bother me. It's just that I'd rather not do it. It's like a piece of candy. You know it will make you fat, but you take it anyway. I don't want to kill something, but I like doing it.

She also revealed strong masochistic tendencies. "I like myself as a person, but physically I don't care what happens to me. I still have myself. I guess I kind of feel like I'm a prisoner in my body.... If someone hurts me I get angry unless it's someone I want to hurt me." When it was pointed out that she was saying these things without any sign of emotion, she indicated that she was in Krishna Consciousness and they taught her not to be emotional. From her description of her interpersonal relationships, it was evident that she withdrew from feelings in an effort to save herself from emotional pain.

> I'll miss [the sniper], but we can't be together forever. I think that's why I don't want to get involved with anybody. We can't be together forever. I think the only way I could love someone is if I know we would never be apart because I need somebody. Every time I've needed somebody, something's happened and they're gone... But I do love people that I know about, who I idolize. Like Charlie, Janis Joplin, Led Zepplin. I don't want to meet them. I think they're perfect and I know they're not.

This girl's psychological test responses underscored her difficulty in forming close, meaningful relationships. Her perceptions, thoughts, and feelings on the Rorschach were almost completely self-centered. Themes of emotional isolation and unconnectedness pervaded her TAT stories. Her sense of distance from others was further demonstrated by her faceless human drawings. It appeared that her sadomasochistic fantasies were her attempt to feel more alive and more in contact with others.

A 12-year-old boy was arrested for forcing a 6-year-old male victim to kiss his penis and buttocks. The 12-year-old appeared very lethargic during the psychological evaluation, displaying absolutely no anxiety, guilt, or embarrassment regarding the incident. He said he knew it was not the right thing to do and he felt the punishment of being in the house for a week was fair. (However, he felt this was also a fair punishment when he wouldn't stop fighting with his brother after his mother told them to stop.) At the time of the incident he displayed some compassion for his victim by releasing him when he started crying, but later he evidenced no concern about possible harmful effects to the victim. He assumed the victim would just "forget about it." His responses to specific questions about the incident revealed that he was motivated by a wish to dominate and degrade another person rather than by any sexual impulse. His mother indicated that he had been subjected to much teasing by his peers because of his large size and he was pretty much of a loner. His mother had long wished he would become less passive and assert himself more, never dreaming he would do it in such a socially unacceptable way. Psychological testing of this boy indicated he was of Normal intelligence. Emotionally, however, he was an island unto himself, blocking out external stimulation, expressing no feelings outwardly, and living in his own inner world of fantasy. He was caught up in fantasy and his perceptions were immature for his age, but he did not give evidence of gross distortions of reality. His retreat from the outside world seemed to be motivated by deep feelings of having been rejected and abused by others. In addition, he was troubled by feelings of inadequacy. Although he occasionally showed a spark of energy to conquer his problems, most of the time he was emotionally drained by them and, feeling completely hopeless, he retreated into passivity. Evidently, the recent incident of dominating and degrading a younger boy was one of his rare attempts to overcome his own inferiority feelings.

A 15-year-old boy was charged with assault to commit rape on a 10-year-old neighbor girl during a game with other children. This boy's appearance and his open, friendly, polite manner during the psychological evaluation made him seem much younger than his age. When questioned about his social life he admitted to being extremely shy and nervous with other kids. He was interested in girls, but he never had a girlfriend and sometimes he got so nervous around them he could not even communicate. He said he talked to himself more than to other people. Psychological testing indicated that his visual-motor functioning was Superior, but his verbal functioning was Dull Normal. Testing also indicated that he had an extremely active imagination and was caught up in his inner world of fantasy. As a result, his reality testing was somewhat impaired. Although his fantasies were not especially primitive or bizarre, he displayed many inaccuracies in his perceptions. In addition, his inner tension was so great he seemed ready to explode, and he harbored many deep-seated sexual concerns. He doubted his masculine identity, was unsure of his sexual role, and felt guilty about his sexual thoughts and actions. His concept of sexuality was childish and he was far from ready to engage in mature sexual behavior. He also was concerned with some intense hostile feelings which he usually kept on the level of fantasy and rarely expressed outwardly. He longed for a better world where people could rise above earthly concerns and he himself was striving to rise above what he considered to be base human instincts. Evidently, his unacceptable sexual and hostile impulses broke through his controls in his recent inappropriate attempt to prove his manhood.

Nonbizarre Behavior of Schizoid Individuals

The acting-out behavior of schizoid individuals is not always bizarre. In some instances their delinquencies appear quite ordinary. However, psychological evaluations of these individuals reveal that their delinquencies stemmed from their difficulty in dealing with reality.

One poorly groomed, apathetic appearing 14-year-old boy
was referred for an evaluation after being charged with a petty
theft from a school locker. During his interview he said: "I'm
trying to put the puzzle together to figure out the future. Like
the locker deal, I wasn't paying too much attention.... While
you're talking I'm thinking of something else." Although he
did not understand the reasons for his theft, it became apparent
in the course of his interview that it was related to his wish to
move from his mother's house to his father's house, a desire
which he explained in terms of his having no friends where his
mother lived, but knowing many people in his father's neighborhood. He avoided discussing his feelings about his parents
themselves. However, separate interviews with his parents
revealed that his mother had a very negative evaluation of him
but wanted him to continue living with her, while his father
overvalued him in completely unrealistic ways, but did not
want the responsibility of taking care of him. Psychological
testing showed this boy to be filled with a great deal of tension
from which he tried to distance himself by fantasizing about
far-off things. Although he exhibited a pronounced tendency to
withdraw from reality, he did not show signs of actual psychosis. His refusal to choose an animal he would most like to be
("I wouldn't exist.... I wouldn't be nothing") apparently
stemmed from his feeling that it was too big a risk for him to
even imagine being something else since he already experienced himself as too far removed from the real world.

A 17-year-old boy who was heavily into drugs was
arrested in a large cocaine deal. Although he had many
ambitions in life, forming close relationships was his highest
goal. Consequently, he was particularly pained by his
increasing sense of estrangement from others. His main
motivation in joining the drug culture was for the social
alliances it offered, and he believed he had a large network of
friends. However, a year before his arrest he began to notice
difficulty in really communicating with others and after his
arrest he felt that most of his friends either double-crossed him
or dropped him. Psychological testing indicated that though he
expressed a strong interest in forming close relationships, he
had little ability to do so at that time. His percepts on the

Rorschach were cold, forbidding, and distant. The major theme of his TAT stories was detachment. He apparently saw the world as a cold, unloving place and he was withdrawing further and further from his goal of close relationships. Although many of his perceptions were idiosyncratic, he did not give evidence of an actual psychosis.

Treatment

Two objectives must be considered at all times in dealing with a schizoid individual who has committed a serious crime: the protection of society and the mental health of this obviously disturbed criminal. Although these two objectives may appear to be contradictory or mutually exclusive, this is not actually the case. While society needs protection from harmful behavior, schizoid individuals, for their own self-esteem and social adaptation, also need to be protected from their unacceptable impulses. Moreover, improving schizoid individuals' mental health so that they will no longer have the need to act out bizarre fantasies is, in the long run, the best protection for society.

The first step for preventing a repetition of the acting-out behavior is close supervision of the individual. Depending upon the circumstances of the case, one of the following alternatives should be taken as soon as the individual is charged with the offense: detention in a juvenile hall, hospitalization in a psychiatric ward, or house arrest. These measures serve the additional purpose of letting the individuals know how seriously their behavior is viewed by society. However, schizoid individuals are so prone to block out reality and are so bland in their emotional reactions that the full significance of what they have done often does not sink in, even after they are detained.

In some cases, the schizoid individuals' tendency to distort reality is aided by their parents' reluctance to confront the situation. For example, one mother said she did not punish her son right away for sexually molesting a younger child because she was so upset that she wanted to wait until she was more rational. However, she never brought the subject up later because of her uneasiness in discussing sex and feelings in general. Thus, in her efforts to calm herself down and in her reticence to deal with feelings, she failed to convey to her son the seriousness of the incident.

In some cases, schizoid individuals block out from their awareness society's reactions to their offenses. For example, even after a true finding had been made in court, one schizoid offender talked as if the charges had been dropped. Then, when he was confronted with the truth, he blandly dismissed the whole matter by claiming ignorance of court procedures.

To ensure that schizoid offenders are facing up to the reality of their situation, it is strongly advised that it be discussed with them in detail.

Psychotherapy is also essential to help these individuals relate more to the real world and less to their fantasies. In fact, helping schizoid offenders improve their social relationships is the best insurance that they will not repeat their acting-out behavior.

The decision about where the therapy should be conducted—in a locked facility, an open-treatment setting, or on an outpatient basis—depends upon an assessment of the seriousness of the crime and the immediate risk of future acting-out behavior. In general, the greater the danger, the further the individual should be removed from the community.

When an out-of-home placement is not deemed necessary for the safety of the community, the resources of the home to help the individual overcome the problem should also be evaluated. If the home environment is seriously lacking or clearly detrimental, out-of-home placement in a treatment facility is advisable.

Chapter 12

INTENSELY EMOTIONAL PSYCHOTICS
AND NEAR PSYCHOTICS

In contrast to the emotionally withdrawn, socially isolated schizoid individuals described in the previous chapter, there are some borderline psychotic, prepsychotic, and psychotic individuals with the opposite problem of overly intense relationships. As a result of their feelings of deprivation and frustrated dependency needs, they reach out to others to fulfill their needs in various inappropriate and self-defeating ways. All the while they deny their feelings and distort reality so that they are not aware of what they are doing. For example, they tend to deny any hostility they may have from a fear of jeopardizing their relationships. But then they project their hostility onto others and end up doing the very thing they feared by angrily reacting to their projected hostility. Their suspicious, untrusting natures also cause them to set up situations to test their friends' loyalty, but the tests they set up are impossible for anyone to pass. At times they assume a greater degree of closeness in a relationship than actually exists and then they are crushed with disappointment when they are forced to face the reality of the situation. As a result of these and many other irrational maneuvers, the stable, lasting relationships for which they yearn constantly elude them. In addition, they sometimes find themselves in trouble with the law. Although the type of legal trouble varies, close examination invariably reveals the source of their trouble to be their irrational ways of trying to fulfill their enormous emotional needs.

Situations Involving Violence

A 15-year-old girl with no prior record was charged with two counts of battery within a month's time. During her evaluation she started off being hostile, surly, and sullen, but after a while become very friendly, pleasant, and cooperative. However, even during her pleasant phase she erupted into several brief tantrums over frustrations that most people would consider minor. She expressed no remorse for the batteries, saying only that her victims got what they deserved for the insulting things they said to her. When her mother (who was present for part of the interview) pointed out how badly they had been hurt, she blamed that on her friend (who took part in the batteries), saying she did not really hurt them but was just teaching them a lesson. When this girl and her mother were asked about the physical discipline she had received as a child, the mother said that she gave the girl only standard spankings, but that the girl's father "is a violent man." The girl added: "My dad used whatever he got his hands on and whenever he felt like it." The mother expressed great surprise upon hearing this. "Until now I never knew of his hitting her except two times." She then described the first incident which occurred when her daughter was five. "She had to stay home a week from school because he hit here in the face with a belt buckle." The other incident she knew of took place the summer before when the girl was staying with her father. In the course of a heated discussion the father knocked the girl unconscious and, according to another daughter who was present, held a loaded gun to her head while she was still unconscious. The mother consulted a lawyer about pressing charges, but learned it was too difficult to prove. This girl moved back with her mother after that incident, but the other daughter stayed with the father even though the mother felt he could turn on that daughter as well. The mother related that during her marriage her husband gave her an "every Saturday night beating and if he felt like it twice during the week." The mother finally left her husband after nearly ten years of marriage. Thus, this girl had to cope with a brutal father and a weak, ineffective mother who avoided facing and dealing with unpleasant realities. As expected, this girl's test responses revealed serious psychological disturbance. Her frequently idiosyncratic, at times bizarre, Rorschach percepts demonstrated her primitive thinking and poor reality testing. They also reflected confusion over bodily intactness and a great deal of anxiety about aggression and physical harm. Although this type of anxiety is usually a contraindication to violent behavior, all sorts of erratic behavior could be expected in this girl because of her extremely disturbed thinking.

A 14½-year-old girl who had been heavily involved with drugs and sex since the age of 13 was sentenced to a girls' rehabilitation center for a second time because of a serious battery on a neighbor girl. She felt the neighbor's repeated insulting remarks about her to others completely justified the beating. In the rehabilitation center she displayed two distinct sides of her personality. Extremely hungry for attention and approval, she responded very warmly to any that was given her. On the other hand, she became very surly and nasty whenever she was blocked in any of her wishes. In a calm frame of mind her statements reflected thoughtfulness and a good set of values. However, when she was in a conflict with someone, she expressed a totally narcissistic, anti-social point of view. While in a good mood she was lively, fun to be with, and very likeable. At other times, she was so self-centered, that it was extremely unpleasant to be with her. Her parents appeared very adoring of her as their long-awaited, only child. However, she indicated she had been abused by both of them. She said her mother hit her with objects about the head for minor infractions of rules and that her father sexually molested her on numerous occasions when she was a young child. One observation of the mother slapping the girl in anger and repeated observations of the father's grossly inappropriate flirting with other girls in the center made her accusations very credible. Psychological testing of this girl showed her to be a bright individual with many inner resources that unfortunately had gone askew. She had a strong interest in and the capacity to reflect upon her experiences, but too often her perceptions of these experiences were distorted by projections of her own negative feelings. She had an active, creative imagination, but too often she ignored outer reality. Although most introspective, imaginative people have good impulse control, it was obvious that hers was very poor. In contrast to her intense involvement with her inner fantasies, she exhibited little sensitivity to external emotional stimuli. Moreover, when she did respond, she did more in terms of her projected fantasies than to the stimuli itself. Clearly, her extreme self-centeredness prevented her from establishing mutually satisfying relationships. She seemed to see the world as a dangerous place and herself as just barely holding on for survival. She also seemed to feel that she had been torn apart by forces beyond her control. She dreamed of finding a secure anchor, a safe harbor, a beautiful paradise where she could have all her wishes fulfilled, but so far she had found none. Sometimes she wished she could pull into a shell like a turtle so she would not have to fight any longer just to survive.

A 16½-year-old girl was sentenced to a girls' rehabilitation center for violation of probation following a petty theft conviction. One week after entering the center she physically attacked another girl and then threatened suicide. A psychological evaluation was requested to determine a suitable placement for her. When she first met the psychologist after arriving in the rehabilitation center, she vividly described her life in Baja California with her "Mexican father, brothers, husband, and baby." When later confronted with the fact that none of these details were in her probation report, she claimed that she never spoke to her probation officer, and her mother did not know all these details or did not want to talk about them. Sometime later, however, she admitted that she had made up these stories to impress the other girls. She also indicated that another reason she made up the stories about her father was that she never met him, and "I want my dad so bad." As for the fight, the girl admitted she probably would not have gotten into it if she had not been upset by her visit with her mother. However, she claimed the other girl provoked the fight by calling her names and she expressed no remorse for her response. Her Rorschach responses revealed serious distortions in her perceptions of reality. Moreover, she failed to see several of the more common percepts even when they were suggested to her. She had difficulty attending to external reality because her thinking was greatly dominated by primitive, morbid, violent fantasies. Furthermore, she demonstrated a striking lack of the kind of constructive imagination needed to delay impulses and consider consequences of behavior. Even though she tended to hold in many of her feelings, it was apparent that when she had a strong impulse to do something, she did it without a second thought.

A 15-year-old girl who violently assaulted a girl at school was observed while locked up to get violently angry whenever she thought someone was saying something bad about her. When first informed that she was referred for a psychological evaluation, she was very negative, even hostile to the idea, saying she was not crazy. However, the next time she saw the psychologist, she pleasantly asked when testing would begin. During the evaluation itself she was cooperative and friendly, even though she was still anxious about what the test would reveal about her. She gave an immediate response to only three of the ten Rorschach cards. The rest of the cards she either rejected or responded to only after a long time. As she carefully examined the cards, she seemed to be searching for the most acceptable percept possible. Despite her apparent attempt to give only conventional responses, a few of her responses were unusual. They showed her to be an individual whose view of the world was highly colored by her own emotions. In particular, she tended to repress her aggressive feelings and project them onto others. Then she could justify her own aggression as a necessary defense against external attack, all the time unaware that the source of most of her aggression was within herself. Her TAT stories conveyed a similar impression. By and large she appeared to relate to others in a pleasant manner and to approach situations in a positive, constructive frame of mind. However, when she saw herself as wronged, she felt completely justified in retaliating to an extent not permitted by society. From her responses on the Animal and Three Wishes tests it appeared that people were very important to her and she yearned for love and intimacy. At the same time, she was wary lest she be dominated and "led around by a leash."

Situations Involving Sexual Molestation

A 13-year-old girl was facing charges of molesting a 4-year-old neighbor child and allegations by younger siblings of sexual abuse over several years. She had also been sexually promiscuous with other males. Her initial greeting to the psychologist was so friendly it almost seemed as if they had already met. She continued to demonstrate her eagerness for close contact throughout the evaluation. At no point did she display anxiety about her situation. In fact, her whole manner seemed very incongruent with the serious charges she was facing. Upon questioning, she vehemently denied the charges and insisted she had proof they were not true. However, her proof consisted of vague statements to the effect that she was not around on the dates of the abuse. In discussing her future placement, she said she was worried she might be placed in a 24-hour (residential treatment) school. On the other hand, she mentioned that she told her mother not to worry, for she was sure she would not be placed in one. Psychological testing indicated that she was of normal intelligence, but that she was prone to peculiear thinking. She seemed to be a severely deprived, pathetically needy girl who was trying to overcome her frustrations through lively, romantic fantasies and cheerful optimism. However, it was apparent from her responses reflecting a paranoid sense of being victimized and a primitive, parasitic need for nurturance, that her defenses were not succeeding. It appeared that this immature girl was still striving for nurturance from her mother as well as from anybody who could possibly give her nurturance or some representation of that need. There was no evidence of strong sexual interest in her test responses. In fact, she displayed extreme sexual immaturity and poor differentiation between the sexes. Evidently, her sexual acting out had been in the service of other, more primitive needs. Like many other young girls, she was probably seeking nurturance, rather than sexual gratification, from older males. In sexually stimulating younger children, she was probably vicariously satisfying her own nurturant needs through a distorted sense of giving.

A 15½-year-old boy with a long history of acting-out behavior and parental rejection was charged with sexually molesting a younger boy. When he was seen for his evaluation he gave the immediate impression of being odd. Whether it was his out-of-style, short haircut, his large, lumpy build and sloppy posture, or his eager, ingratiating friendliness, typical of a much younger child, this boy definitely seemed out of step with his peers. His responses to questions about the incident revealed that although he was ashamed of his homosexual activity, was determined to stop it, and wanted the whole matter quickly forgotten, he had no understanding of the seriousness of molesting a child. It was as if he saw himself on the same level as the child and he regarded his behavior as nothing more than "naughty" sexual experimentation. He seemed to have absolutely no awareness of how intimidating he must have been to the child, due to his greater size and strength, as well as the threats he made to force compliance. Psychological testing revealed severe psychological disturbance in this youth. While he did not totally misperceive the form qualities in the Rorschach inkblots, he displayed the kind of loose associations and fluid thinking normally seen only in dream images. His inappropriate handling of emotional stimuli further demonstrated his difficulty in logically and realistically organizing his perceptions. His TAT stories also reflected severe emotional problems. In one story he so vividly portrayed feelings of failure and humiliation, it was obvious he was talking about himself. In another story that started off fairly controlled, he got carried away with a sadomasochistic theme. The ghostlike, robotlike, outer space appearance of his human drawings suggested that he saw himself as not completely of this world. Feelings of being dead and empty inside were also suggested by his drawing of a tree.

Situations Involving Stealing

An 11-year-old boy who was involved in repeated thefts and burglaries related to the psychologist in an appealingly open, friendly, cheerful manner. At the same time he displayed marked immaturity by his thumbsucking and his failure to recognize boundaries. While returning from the playroom to the psychologist's office, he suddenly opened a closed door to another private office just to see what was in there. Then, during his evaluation he practically crawled on top of the desk to get in closer contact with the psychologist. He indicated that he wanted to stop stealing because of the expense to his parents in hiring lawyers, etc., but, he added, "It's pretty hard once you got the habit in you." Psychological testing showed this boy to be severely disturbed with very poor reality testing. Primitive, bizarre fantasies dealing with internal organs, bodily functions, illness, and decay permeated his Rorschach responses which, incidentally, bore little or no relationship to the form of the inkblots. In his human figure drawing he enclosed the entire body, including the hands and the feet, with a protective covering. Thus, he displayed tremendous anxiety about the intactness of his own body, as if he sensed that he was beginning to disintegrate and he needed to do whatever he could to keep from falling apart completely. His morbid preoccupation with violence, murder, and death in his TAT stories suggested that he felt under constant attack. One story in particular vividly portrayed his identification with victims of violence: "This boy, he went to school and the kids beat up on him and he ran home and he's so tired, he fell on the ground and fainted and he's crying and he feels like running away from home." This boy's behaviorally observed failure to recognize boundaries was further demonstrated in the testing. On the Rorschach he repeatedly joined two cards to form a whole picture and on the TAT he started one story by describing what was happening in the picture and ended by placing himself in the situation and describing personal experiences completely unrelated to the picture. In another TAT story he jumped from one point in time to another and considered the same picture to be representing both. It was evident from his poor reality testing and his inability to maintain boundaries that this boy's stealing was beyond his control, as he suggested in one of his remarks.

A 17-year-old boy was referred for a psychological evaluation because of his repeated thefts and burglaries. He was first seen with his father. During the interview he sat quietly while his father angrily enumerated all the things the boy had done wrong and all the things the father had done to try to correct the situation. The father appeared to be a strong-minded, hardworking, responsible individual with deep convictions about right and wrong. The boy did not deny anything his father said and did not try to defend himself in any way. In his individual interview the boy expressed an opinion that his father did not have to go into all that detail to make him look so bad. He went on to say that he feels his father is too strict and treats him like a little kid. On the other hand, he expressed a great deal of admiration for his father and from everything he said it was apparent that he felt woefully lacking in comparison with his father. Testing showed this boy to be functioning intellectually in the Low-Average range and possibly suffering from minimal brain damage. Severe emotional disturbance was also evident in the test data. His perceptions of reality were highly unconventional and, in some instances, bizarre. It appeared from his responses that he was so filled with tension, he felt ready to explode or fall apart. He also seemed to be bothered by feelings of being lost, lonely, and confused. For example, in response to one Rorschach card which is normally seen as two people engaged in a cooperative activity, he saw: "A bunch of islands invaded by UFOs." Several of his TAT stories confirmed the psychologist's impression that despite his delinquent behavior, his values were basically nondelinquent. He displayed a high need for achievement and a belief in hard work. It appeared that this boy was acting out in delinquent ways and doing everything he could to alienate his father due to a deep sense of inadequacy to live up to his father's standards which he respected highly.

Situations Involving Relatively Mild Acting-Out Behavior

A 17-year-old boy who had run away innumerable times from many different placements could not understand why the authorities would not let him be free. However, it was quickly obvious to the most casual observer that he was seriously disturbed and he was always picked up for vagrancy within a few days of running away. This boy was extremely fanciful in his responses to the Rorschach. At times it seemed that he might be consciously playing with fantasy the way some stream of consciousness writers purposely regress in the "service of the ego" to express deep feelings. At other times there was no doubt that his fantasies were overtaking him, his reality testing was disappearing, and he was becoming fully immersed in psychotic thought. For example:

> I see this as a mermaid maiden and these bears are the California state flag. So, therefore, what I am saying is this mermaid is my mother. These bears, which are the symbol of California, are the carpet in my mother's house, like the white fur of her carpet. . . . This here is a hippie-freak, anti-Christ, Charles Manson. This is his crown of glory, the symbol of Judas Iscariot. I think it's symbolically out of space. I think these are Charlie's favorite colors. Green means he is a very giving person. Yellow means he is a very bright dude, bright personality. Orange is extract. Orange means he is a very giving person. It could mean a lot of things. It could mean he is odyssey for space.

A 12-year-old girl arrested for false identification to a police officer insisted to the psychologist that she was 13 even though her records showed she was 12. The issue of her age was also raised in the courtroom and the conclusion was that she was 12. When later confronted with this, she explained that she figures her birthday the Chinese way. Upon questioning this girl denied having any problems whatsoever despite her mother's statements to the effect that she was completely beyond control. This girl refuted her mother's opinion by stating: "When I want to get along with her, I get along fine." Nevertheless, her responses to several specific questions indicated that something was seriously awry in her home situation. ["When do you want to get along with her?"] "When I can talk to her.... She never has time to sit and talk.... I get along with her when I see her. I'm usually at a friend's house or the park till it's time for me to come in.... I don't usually eat dinner at all. My mom wants me to, but I don't want to.... I don't like being at home. It's a bore. I fall asleep. I like to be out running, playing.... I like to be on my own." When the possibility of an out-of-home placement was raised, this girl became very agitated. "I'm not going anywhere. If I do, I'll break things.... punch walls.... I'll make everybody else crazy. I'll punch everybody out.... I can control myself just as much as I want to." Psychological testing showed this girl to be a fearful, unhappy individual with impaired reality testing. Her Rorschach was filled with unpleasant percepts that often did not match the form of the blots. She appeared to have great interest in, yet great anxiety about, interpersonal relationships. She seemed to feel that she was living a nightmare, alone and adrift in a world of terrors, with no solid safe ground to stand on and no one to depend upon. She sought solace from everyday unhappiness through grandiose fantasies of the future.

A 17-year-old boy was arrested after a fight with his mother in which he slapped her and stole $2.00 from her purse. He was placed in juvenile hall and his mother was refusing to have him home again. He indicated that he wanted to live at home until he reaches the age of 22 or 23 so he can save money to invest and then be set for life. He stated: "I don't really care if I get along with my mom. I'm just looking to my future. We haven't made passionate gestures for three years." Upon questioning it became clear that he saw no distinction between the words "passionate" and "affectionate." He said he and his mother were really close when he was younger. He felt they started having problems when he became a teenager and she did not want to let him do the things he wanted to do. In the recent incident he had asked her for a loan of $2.00 for gas so he could immediately return some money he owed to someone else. At first she agreed, but then refused. He felt she had no good reason to refuse the loan, especially since he would be repaying her that afternoon when he got his paycheck. In anger he grabbed her purse and took the $2.00 from it. Then, according to him, she seized the purse and started hitting him over the head with it and kicking him all over. He responded by hitting her across the face, whereupon she ordered him out of the house. Psychological testing showed this boy of Bright Normal or higher intelligence to be struggling with many problems which were overwhelming him. Tremendous ambivalence and conflict permeated his responses. In some situations he tried to defend against conflict through a reaction formation which expressed the socially approved side of his conflict. However, in various subtle and not so subtle ways he inadvertently revealed the other side of the conflict. In other situations he could not even decide which path he wanted to take. As soon as he tried to resolve a conflict by moving in one direction, he immediately reversed his direction, only to switch over and over again. With all his ambivalence it was very difficult for him to know what he actually felt and who he really was. In addition, he exhibited a marked lack of clarity in his perceptions of the world around him. His widespread confusion was also evident in his peculiar language patterns. Other signs of his psychotic potential were his tendency at times to be overly concrete and at other times to make sweeping generalizations. The test data further indicated that this boy was filled with hurt, anger, and a deep sense of inferiority stemming from his perception of his parents as rejecting him. He desperately tried to overcome these feelings through intensely ambitious strivings, which he was incapable of fulfilling because his functioning was so erratic and his strivings so grandiose and unrealistic. He appeared tied to his mother in an extremely hostile-dependent relationship. He seemed to feel that they were engaged in a serious tug-of-war for survival and, at the same time, they were dependent on each other for survival. In other words, if either let go, they would both be destroyed. So there was no way either could really win. Afraid to give in and afraid to let go, they stubbornly continued locking horns. Evidently, the incident which led to his arrest was just one of many in his unhealthy struggle with his mother.

Treatment

Since the unacceptable behavior of psychotic and near psychotic individuals is so often beyond their rational control, punishment will have little, if any, impact on their behavior. What these individuals need is intensive psychological treatment to learn how to fulfill their needs in acceptable ways so they will no longer feel compelled to act them out in various inappropriate and illegal ways. The question of whether the treatment should be conducted on an inpatient or outpatient basis depends on several factors, including the seriousness of the offender's threat to the community and himself, as well as the acuteness or chronicity of the emotional disturbance. In general, the more serious the threat, and the more acute the disturbance, the more necessary is inpatient treatment.

Chapter 13

ANTISOCIAL PERSONALITIES

There is a diagnostic category, variously referred to as psychopathic, sociopathic, or antisocial personality, that is often viewed with greater dread than any other diagnosis. The *Diagnostic and Statistical Manual of Mental Disorders*, published by the American Psychiatric Association, describes the antisocial personality as follows:

> This term is reserved for individuals who are basically unsocialized and whose behavior patterns brings them repeatedly into conflict with society. They are incapable of significant loyalty to individuals, groups, or social values. They are grossly selfish, callous, irresponsible, impulsive, and unable to feel guilt or to learn from experience and punishment. Frustration tolerance is low. They tend to blame others or offer plausible ratiohalizations for their behavior. A mere history of repeated legal or social offenses is not sufficient to justify this diagnosis.

Even though the overall functioning of psychotics is much more deteriorated than that of antisocial personalities, there is in the case of acute psychosis always the chance of recovery, either spontaneously or through treatment. The prognosis for antisocial personalities, on the other hand, is extremely pessimistic. Moreover, though chronic psychotics have little hope of full recovery, most of them are harmless and their most offensive behavior is usually controllable through medication. Antisocial personalities, on the other hand, repeatedly inflict great harm on others, and their behavior is not usually controllable through medication.

In the case of organic brain damage, major portions of the brain, including those affecting intelligence and personality, are often intact. Moreover, with time and training, there is always the possibility that the intact areas will take over the functions of the damaged areas. Antisocial personality traits, on the other hand, pervade the entire personality.

Though mentally retarded individuals are severely limited in their intellectual functioning and antisocial personalities are often quite bright, retarded individuals are capable of warm, loving relationships, something completely beyond the capacity of antisocial personalities. While it may appear on the surface that antisocial personalities get along well with others because they are often quite charming, upon close examination it is apparent that to them people are merely objects to be used, manipulated, and discarded at will. They do not know what it is to genuinely care about another human being.

The other remarkable thing about antisocial personalities is that many of their criminal activities are seemingly purposeless, motivated by no apparent frustration, anger, need, or greed. In other words, they often hurt others just "for the hell of it," without even considering the risk to themselves, let alone to others. As a result of their lack of normal anxiety to warn them of impending danger, they eventually get in trouble. In a classic study of these personalities, *Mask of Sanity*, Cleckly vividly depicts the senselessness of much of the antisocial personalities' behavior.

In my clinical experience I have seen many individuals with various antisocial personality traits to varying degrees, but scarcely any who fully encompass all the traits or who are totally lacking in normal feelings. For example, one 15-year-old girl, charged with armed robbery, exhibited gross callousness with regard to the well-being of people in general, but expressed a great deal of fondness for her young niece, thereby demonstrating at least some capacity for warm relationships. In another case, a 16-year-old boy who blithely violated innumerable laws and social rules of behavior commented before going to prison that he was afraid he might get into a fight there and end up killing someone. He said he did not want to do that because he never wants to have that awful feeling again after killing someone. Thus, he exhibited the presence of at least some conscience. In some cases the presence of underlying sadness holds out hope that the person displaying antisocial personality traits can be reached in therapy. A 14-year-old girl in custody for attempting to run over the owner of the car she stole, openly admired a sniper for having the guts to kill. Moreover, she could not understand why everyone was so upset about the incident. As she saw it, ''We all have to die sometime.'' Her underlying feelings of depression were revealed, however, by her statement that she did not particularly care if she lived or died. In another case, a 14-year-old boy, charged with sexually molesting a younger girl, expressed intense annoyance at the inconvenience of being on house arrest for several weeks before the trial. He initially denied the charges, but then admitted them. However, he exhibited absolutely no regret for his behavior or concern for his victim. These reactions paralleled one of his TAT stories in which a murderer's only concern was to dispose of the body as quickly as possible to avoid detection. In his utter lack of conscience and his completely narcissistic orientation, this boy certainly qualified for the antisocial personality diagnosis. However, it appeared from his history of abusive parental treatment and rejection by peers that he must also have a lot of underlying sadness in him. In all likelihood, his callousness was a defense against feeling the sadness in him for the things he had suffered in life.

Instead of viewing the antisocial personality diagnosis as an all-or-none category, it seems more useful to view it as a personality pattern present to a greater or lesser extent in different people. Although the prognosis is admittedly poor for those with strong antisocial traits, therapy should be attempted, particularly in the younger population, in the hope that the antisocial features of the personality are not totally dominant or fixed and that other more desirable features of the personality can be strengthened. Besides, there is usually a limit to how long these individuals can be locked up for a particular crime and, since they are rarely improved by the prison experience, this is all the more reason to attempt psychological treatment.

The fact that treatment of antisocial personalities can be effective was amply demonstrated in the following two cases. In the first, a 12-year-old boy who had been known to the police since the age of eight for repeated shoplifting had been diagnosed by several psychiatrists and psychologists as markedly psychopathic with absolutely no feelings of anxiety or guilt. It was noted in his history that his father, who had been in prison several times, had taught him to steal. The prognosis for this boy was very gloomy. However, after five months in a 24-hour school the boy seemed greatly changed. In contrast to his former attitude of not caring about anything, he displayed considerable anxiety about his performance on the tests and his future. He said he wanted to do well to show he was ready to return home. He also indicated that he was tired of being at "the bottom of the heap," as the 24-hour school director had repeatedly told him he was. His new drive for achievement was also demonstrated by the dramatic improvement in his reading (several grades progress in less than a year). This boy indicated he did not like the director at the 24-hour school because he was constantly after him to talk. However, he admitted that all that talking got him thinking and he began to realize things he never realized before. For example, he now believed it is not right for him to steal because he would not want anybody stealing from him. The fact that this was not a phony or superficial change of attitude was repeatedly demonstrated in the test data. Whereas he had previously been extremely impulsive, he now exercised such extreme caution in controlling his impulses that he appeared to be quite obsessive-compulsive. Though he needed further treatment to help him become more at ease in controlling his impulses, it was clear that his newly developed obsessive-compulsive traits were a vast improvement over his previous antisocial traits. As an obsessive-compulsive he could function in society; as an antisocial personality he would spend his life in and out of criminal institutions.

A wild and rebellious 14-year-old girl was extremely difficult to manage in a rehabilitation center. Unlike most of the girls there who quickly settle into the routine, realizing that the sooner they did, the sooner they would be permitted to leave, this girl continued for a long time to behave as if she were a law unto herself, ignoring every rule not to her liking, regardless of consequences. No matter what new restriction or new punishment was imposed, she acted as if she did not care. Psychological testing was requested for suggestions of new ways to handle her. Her test responses were classically anti-social, reflecting cold, contemptuous attitudes toward others, an ugly view of life, and very poor impulse control. However, there were some indications of underlying hurt due to a sense of being rejected by her mother. The girl readily admitted to having these feelings which she said she had pushed deep down inside her because they hurt so much there was nothing she could do about them. She was very open to the suggestion of counseling with her mother and her mother also agreed to participate. Although the mother was an extremely self-centered individual, she did make an effort to become more responsive to her daughter. After several months of counseling during which time there were noticeable improvements in this girl's relationship with her mother, and in her behavior on the unit, she was retested. This time the clinical picture was entirely different. He perceptions of reality were more conventional and her impulse control was much better. In addition, she demonstrated the capacity to empathize with the feelings of others and to express warm feelings of her own. In other words, she had become socialized, to a much greater degree than she had previously been.

Treatment

There seems to be two main approaches to treating individuals with antisocial personalities. Therapy emphasizing psychodynamics attempts to get them in touch with their underlying feelings of loneliness and sadness in order to motivate them to want to change their self-defeating behavior patterns. On the other hand, therapy emphasizing reasoning and behavior modification techniques focuses on the learning of socially adaptive behavior. Obviously both approaches are needed. In order for therapy to be effective it is necessary to both motivate a desire for change and to teach how change can be accomplished.

Chapter 14

PARENTAL PATTERNS OF BEHAVIOR
IN FAMIILIES OF DELINQUENTS

The cases described in the previous chapters offer much evidence to support the widespread belief that parents play a significant role in the delinquencies of their children. This is not to say that parents are totally or even primarily to blame for their children's behavior. There are also societal factors and inborn traits influencing behavior. In addition, there is the elusive element of individual choice which dramatically distinguishes people in ways that innate differences, family background, and life experiences cannot explain. It is obvious that all these factors interact in varoius ways to produce delinquent behavior and the relative weight of each varies with the subject.

In some cases the role of the parents is not at all clear. The juvenile offender may protectively guard his parents from blame by denying the existence of any problems within the family that might have prompted his acting out. The parents may also be very defensive about looking at their contribution to their child's delinquency. Nevertheless, in my experience working with delinquent girls and their families in a rehabilitation center, even the most staunchly defended families eventually reveal significant problems. It should be noted, however, that this is not necessarily true of families of delinquent boys. Delinquency is much more common among boys than girls. In my experience the ratio of boys to girls detained in juvenile detention and rehabilitation facilities is approximately 7:1. Since delinquency is less deviant behavior among boys than among girls, it is possible that it is not as strong an indication of problems in boys as it is in girls. This thinking is certainly in line with the observations of many probation officers that delinquent girls are as a rule far more emotionally disturbed than delinquent boys.

It should be noted that regardless of whether parents are aware of their mistakes, by and large these mistakes stem from limitations within the parents and are not intentional. Often the parents themselves received inadequate parental care and, as a result, never developed a clear idea of what good parenting entails. In other cases, the parents are aware of their children's needs, but are so overwhelmed with problems in their own lives that they have little in the way of energy or resources to give their children. Some parents are too weak to set any limits on their children's behavior. The opposite is true in other cases where the parents try very hard to set limits, but are too rigid in their expectations and not sufficiently in tune with their children's feelings. Then there are some parents who transmit to their children their distorted views of the world, their immature coping mechanisms, or their antisocial values. It is obvious that there are many different kinds of parental behavior that can lead to juvenile delinquency. This chapter focuses on some of the patterns I have repeatedly observed in my work with families of juvenile offenders.

Lack of Consistent Parenting

Some parents are so wrapped up in their own needs that they have little to give their children. They might verbally express love and concern, but in their behavior they repeatedly let their children down in various important ways. They might make promises only to break them or they might be so insensitive they completely ignore their children's feelings. In some cases they do not even provide the basic care our society sees as the right of every child. An obvious example of this insufficient attention to a child's physical needs, can, if extreme, warrant removal of the child from the home. Inadequate protection and supervision, though usually less obvious to the outside observer, can be just as emotionally devastating to a child.

Parents who inadequately protect and supervise their child are following the course of least resistance without bothering to stop and consider the long-range consequences. For example, in cases where one parent is abusing or sexually molesting a child, the other parent often ignores the situation to keep the family intact, even though the family is operating in very harmful ways. Another example is when parents indiscriminately grant their teenager the privileges of adulthood in order to avoid any unpleasant confrontation.

When children perceive their parents as uncaring, the children look elsewhere for the nurturance and self-validation they lack at home. While some children find this nurturance and self-validation in positive sources, many find it in relationships and activities that are destructive. Of course, the more disruptive the child's behavior, the more the parents withdraw from him or her. While most observers sympathize with either the child or the parent, it should be recognized that both experience a great deal of emotional pain in the relationship. Besides, though parents and children are individually responsible for their behavior in a given situation, both parents and children are often thrust into situations not of their choosing, and the mistakes they make in these situations are usually reactions to stress, not something they deliberately plan.

Parents of juvenile offenders who do not provide adequate care of their children need a lot of support and guidance to improve their parenting skills. If they are unwilling or unable to change, out-of-home placement of their children should be considered as a way of preventing future delinquencies.

Overly Strict Parents

Although it is expected that parental rules vary, some parents make the mistake of setting extremely high standards of behavior compared to the norm for their community. Then they rigidly try to enforce their rules regardless of their children's feelings. These are the parents who think in absolute, black and white terms, who do not know the meaning of the word compromise. They believe that what was good for them is good for their children, without taking into account differences in time and locale.

While these overly strict parents may succeed in enforcing their rules with some of their children, all too often, at least one, and sometimes more, of their children rebel. When their children subsequently get into trouble with the authorities, these parents are truly flabbergasted. They have taught their children right from wrong and they themselves have been models of good behavior. Therefore, they cannot understand how any child of theirs could have gone so far astray. Moreover, since these parents are so rigid and absolute in their thinking, they sincerely believe they have done everything they could have done for their children and they cannot imagine what mistakes they could have possibly made. They tend to regard their troublesome child as some sort of alien who has mysteriously popped up in their midst. They see absolutely no connection between the misbehavior of their errant child and their own rigid, controlling behavior.

Furthermore, since these parents are so sincere in the essential rightness of their beliefs, they are often able to convince the authorities of their point of view. Anybody who has prolonged contact with these families, however, eventually dis- covers some of the parents' behavior that has negatively affected their children. In one such case it was discovered that a father, who had appeared to many probation officers to be a model parent, had repeatedly spanked his 15-year-old daughter on her bare bottom for misbehavior most parents would not even consider especially serious. It was no wonder that this girl started running away from home and eventually got into trouble with the law.

Parental strictness usually centers on the issues of freedom and responsibility. The child may feel unfairly restricted, unfairly burdened, or both. If teenagers are treated like children with few privileges and few responsibilities, they may or may not accept the situation. In the opposite case, if teenagers are treated like adults with many privileges and many responsibilities, there may also be a problem.

There is bound to be trouble, however, if a teenager is treated like a child with few privileges and like an adult with many responsibilities. It is only natural that the teenager will resent the situation and rebel in some way. Parents in these situations usually do not realize how unfair they are being. They believe they are raising their children the way they were raised: to respect and obey their parents, without question, and to expect few privileges. The point they overlook is that when they were growing up mothers usually stayed at home and did the housework, whereas nowadays, with many mothers working outside the home, children are being expected to do more and more housework than ever before. There are families in which children bitterly resent that they are required to do housework as soon as they get home from school and perhaps even prepare supper before their parents' arrival so their parents can have time to relax after a hard day of work. The children feel that they too deserve some relaxation when they get home from their work at school. Then when they relax at the time their parents expect them to be studying, they find that their parents can't understand why they are not better students.

Counseling is advisable in these cases to help parents become more reasonable in their expectations and demands. If parents are resistant to change, out-of-home placement of the children may be necessary to prevent future delinquencies.

Parental Loss of Emotional Control Under Stress

Many well-meaning parents try to be loving and reasonable with their children and manage fairly well under ordinary circumstances. However, stressful situations overwhelm them and they end up saying and doing things that are very damaging to their children. These are the parents who tend to over-react at the first sign of trouble from their children. Instead of calmly discussing the situation to try to understand why their child is misbehaving and to figure out steps to prevent future incidents, they lash out in ways that actually increase the likeli-

hood of future acting out. For example, in the midst of a conflict with her daugher, one mother screamed: "I hate you. I
hate you. Get out of here." Later, after the mother had calmed
down, she waited for her daughter to return home. However,
the daughter, believing her mother meant what she said, stayed
away until she was picked up by the police. In another case, a
father similarly lost control during an argument with his adoptive daughter and told her the biggest mistake of his life was
adopting her. This girl said she knew her father did not really
mean it, but her grooming and behavior reflected extremely
low self-esteem and she claimed to have no feelings whatsoever
for her adoptive parents.

Interestingly enough, the parents who lose control of their
emotions in these damaging ways are often the very parents
who complain about their children's impulsiveness. Considering the example of poor self-control in their parents, the
children's lack of self-control is not at all surprising. Fortu-
nately, many of these parents can see the connection between
their behavior and that of their children's when it is pointed out
to them. However, this does not mean they are automatically
capable of changing their behavior once they are aware of its
damaging effects.

These parents usually need therapy to improve their emotional controls so they can handle situations more maturely. If
the parents are resistant to therapy, out-of-home placement for
their acting-out child may be necessary to prevent future
delinquencies.

Overly Bland Parental Reactions to Child's Misbehavior

Some parents are diametrically opposite from overreactive
parents in that they fail to react at all to their children's misbehavior. Because of emotional shock or a feeling of inadequacy
relating to their children's acting out, they simply withdraw
from the situation and do not say anything to correct or teach
their children. They pass on the parental responsibility of controlling their children's behavior to other authorities, thereby
missing the opportunity to convey their attitudes and values to

their children. Lacking feedback from their parents about their behavior, these children never fully grasp the seriousness of what they have done and they never absorb their parents' socially constructive values.

These parents need therapy to become more comfortable with their feelings and better able to express them in socially appropriate ways.

Parental Teaching of Socially Unacceptable Attitudes and Behavior

Because of their own deeply rooted socially deviant attitudes or their unsuccessful coping mechanisms, some parents teach their children attitudes and behavior that gets them into trouble.

Some parents convey an attitude that the world is out to get you and it is better to "take" than to be "taken." They also teach their children to take revenge upon anyone who has done them wrong. Of course, what constitutes a wrong is open to individual interpretation and may include such normally accepted or ignored incidents as an unintentional slight or a necessary reprimand. Likewise, what constitutes "justifiable" revenge is also open to individual interpretation and may include anything from harassment to bodily harm.

Instead of teaching their children to try to get along with others—or, if they can't get along with someone, to avoid that person—some parents encourage their children to fight back for any provocation, even verbal insults. Moreover, the threats of some parents to beat up their child if that child loses a fight makes many initially timid children extremely aggressive.

Some parents who are themselves extremely resentful of any and all authority teach their children to disrespect outside authorities. This lays the groundwork for behavior that brings children into conflict with society. When society reacts by imposing more and more restraints, the child's resentment of authority and acting-out behavior are heightened.

Finally, in various subtle and not so subtle ways, some parents teach their children to cheat and steal to get the things they want instead of teaching them to work and save for those things.

Thus, parents are often very instrumental in preparing their children for irresponsible behavior. In many ways these children are the hardest to treat. Their behavior goes hand in hand with the values their parents have taught them, even though it clashes with the rest of society. Winning the children over to another point of view can be very difficult, particularly if they are strongly attached to their parents and feel loyally bound to adhere to their parents' teachings. In these cases, it is often worthwhile to attempt counseling with the parents to see if their children's trouble with the law makes them willing to convey more socially responsible attitudes and ideas to their children.

Family Crises

In some instances the delinquent child is responding to a particular set of stressful circumstances within the family, rather than a long-established pattern. Such circumstances include severe illness or death of one of the family members, sexual molestation by a family member, threatened or actual divorce of the parents, or the introduction of a stepparent into the family constellation (particularly when the stepparent is deemed totally unacceptable by virtue of his or her young age, or when the natural parent fully relinquishes his or her authority over the children to the stepparent). The responses to these circumstances include running away to escape the situation, engaging in some criminal activity to cause removal from the home, acting-out resentment through destruction of property, and direct expression of anger through violent behavior.

Need for Treatment of Family

While this chapter focuses on desired changes within the parents to combat their children's delinquencies, it must be understood that once a pattern of acting-out behavior begins, a whole system is often set up within the family that maintains that behavior. Therefore, while counseling and/or therapy with the parents, on the one hand, and the juvenile offender, on the other, can get at underlying causes of the problem behavior, it is not always sufficient to remedy the situation. Family sessions are usually also required to work out the family conflicts.

References

Alexander, F., & Healy, W. *Roots of crime*. Montclair, N.J.: Patterson Smith, 1969 (orig. copyright, 1935).

American Psychiatric Association. *Diagnostic and statistical manual of mental disorders II*. Washington, D.C.: American Psychiatric Association, 1968.

Andrew, J.M. Violence Among Delinquents by Family Intactness and Size. *Social Biology*, 1978, *25*, 179-195.

Andrew, J.M. Violence and poor reading. *Criminology*, 1979, *17*, 3, 361-365.

Austin, R. Race, father absence, and female delinquency. *Criminology*, February, *15*, No. 4, 487-504.

Brown, W., & Simpson, B. "Confrontation of Self Through Outdoor Challenge: Pennsylvania's Outdoor Experience for Juvenile Offenders." *Behavioral Disorders*, 1976, *2*, 41-48.

Cernkovich, S. Value orientations and delinquency involvement. *Criminology*, 1978a, *15*, 4, 443-458.

Cernkovich, S. Evaluating two models of delinquency causation: Structural theory and control theory. *Criminology*, 1978b, *16*, 3, 335-352.

Cleckly, H. *The mask of sanity*. St. Louis: C.V. Mosley, 1941.

Cohen, A.K. *Delinquent boys*. New York: Free Press, 1955.

Dudycha, G. Juvenile delinquency. *Psychology for Law Enforcement Officers*. Springfield, IL: Charles C. Thomas, 1955, 249-271.

Eagly, A. H., & Anderson, P. Sex role and attitudinal correlates of desired family size. *Journal of Applied Social Psychology*, 1974, *4*, 151-164.

Eaton, J., & Polk, K. *Measuring delinquency*. Pittsburgh: University of Pittsburgh Press, 1961.

Erickson, M., & Jensen, G. Delinquency is still group behavior: Toward revitalizing the group premise in the sociology of deviance. *Journal of Criminal Law and Criminology*, 1977, *68*, 2, 263-273.

Friday, P., & Hage, J. Youth Crime in Postindustrial Societies. *Criminology*, 1976, *14*, 3, 347-368.

Friday, P., & Halsey, J. Patterns of social relationships and youth crime: Social integration and prevention. In P.C. Friday & V.L. Stewart (Eds.), *Youth crime and juvenile justice*. New York: International Perspectives, Praeger, 1977.

Glasser, W. *Reality Therapy*. New York: Harper, 1965.

Glueck, S., & Glueck, E. *Juvenile delinquents grown up*. New York: The Commonwealth Fund, 1940.

Hepburn, J. Testing alternative models of delinquent causation. *Journal of Criminal Law and Criminology*, 1976, *67*, 4, 450-460.

Jenkins, R. The Runaway Reaction. In W.L. McCraney (Ed.), *Readings in criminal psychology*. New York: M.S.S. Information Corp., 1972.

Kapsis, R. Residential succession and delinquency: A test of Shaw and McKay's theory of cultural transmission. *Criminology*, 1978, *15*, 4, 450-486.

Lewis, D., Balla, D., Shanok, S., & Snell, L. Delinquency, parental psychopathology, and parental criminality, clinical and epidemiological findings. *Journal of the American Academy of Child Psychiatry*, 1976, *15*, 4, 665-678.

Lewis, D.O. Diagnostic evaluation of the juvenile offender. *Child Psychiatry and Human Development*, 1976, *6*, 4, 198-213.

McCord, W., & McCord, J. *The psychopath*. Princeton: D. Van Nostrand, 1964.

Nettler, G. *Explaining crime*. New York: McGraw-Hill, 1974.

Rankin, J. Investigating the interrelations among social control variables and conformity. *Journal of Criminal Law and Criminology*, 1976, *67*, 4, 470-480.

Robins, L.N., West, P.A., & Herjanic, B.L. Arrests and delinquency in two generations: A study of black urban families and their children. *Journal of Child Psychology and Psychiatry*, 1975, *16*, 125-140.

Saunders, G.R., & Davies, M.B. The validity of the Jesness inventory with British delinquents. *British Journal of Social Clinical Psychology*, 1976, *15*, 33-39.

Shore, M. Psychological theories of the causes of antisocial behavior. *Crime and Delinquency*, 1971, *17*, 4, 456-468.

Sorrells, J. Kids who kill. *Crime and delinquency*, 1977, *23*, 3, 312-320.

Taylor, T., & Watt, D. The relation of deviant symptoms and behavior in a normal population to subsequent delinquency and maladjustment. *Psychological medicine*, 1977, *7*, 1, 163-169.

Truax, C. Degree of negative transference occurring in group psychotherapy and client outcome in juvenile delinquents. In McCraney (Ed.), *Readings in criminal psychology*. New York: M.S.S. Information Corp., 1972.

Yochelson, S., & Samenow, S. *The criminal personality* (Vols. I & II). Jason Aronson: New York, 1976.

INDEX

Robins, .N. 10

Samenow, S., 19, 25
Saunders, G.R., 12
"Scared Straight," 20
Schizoid personalities, 80-88
    nonbizarre behavior of, 85-87
    compared to schizophrenics, 80
School adjustment, 22-23
Seclusion, 64
Self-esteem, low, 46
Self-image, poor, 47, 61
Sexual
    abuse, 94
    molestation, 94-96
Shore, M., 13
Simpson, B., 19
Society, conflict with, 114
Sociopathic (see antisocial)
Stealing, 96
Structural theories, 18
    compared to control
        theories, 18
Supervision by probation
    officer, 26
Sutherland model, 14, 16

Tantrums, 90
Test anxiety, 78
"Testing Alternate Modes of
Delinquent Causation"
    (Hepburn), 15
Tests
    Animal, 94
    psychological (see psychological
        testing)
    Three Wishes, 94
Thematic Apperception Test
    (TAT), 34, 35, 47, 56, 58, 69,
    76, 77, 83, 86, 95, 96, 97, 104
Therapy,
    family, 45
    individual, 45

Thumbsucking, 96
Treatment, 18-20, 21
    appropriate, 24-26
    arrest, 87
    behavior modification
        techniques of, 107
    change of environment, 70
    confinement, 53, 65
    counseling, 65, 70
    court appearance, 65
    detention, 87
    for family, 115-116
    hospitalization, 87
    inpatient-outpatient, 101
    institutionalization, 79
    intensive
        psychological, 101
        residential, 54, 79, 94
    leisure time, structured, 70
    out-of-home placement, 87
    probation, 65
    psychoanalysis, 19
    psychotherapy, 65, 87
    recommended, 26
    supervision of, 87

"Value Orientations and
    Delinquency
    Involvement" (Cernkovich),
    18
Violence, 90
    history of, 56
Violent assault, 93
Vulnerability, sense of, 60-65

West, P.A., 10
Withdrawl of affection, 13

Yochelson, S., 19, 25